GRADUATE PSYCHOMETRIC TEST WORKBOOK

ADVANCED LEVEL

MIKE BRYON

KOGAN PAGE

Publisher's Note

Every possible effort has been made to ensure that the information contained in this book is accurate at the time of going to press, and the publishers and authors cannot accept responsibility for any errors or omissions, however caused. No responsibility for loss or damage occasioned to any person acting, or refraining from action, as a result of the material in this publication can be accepted by the editor, the publisher or any of the authors.

First Indian Edition 2008

Kogan Page India Private Limited
4737/23 Ansari Road,
Daryaganj
New Delhi 110 002

This edition is for sale in Indian subcontinent only. Not for export elsewhere.

ISBN-10: 81-7554-398-1
ISBN-13: 978-81-7554-398-0

Published by Vinod Vasishtha for Kogan Page India Private Limited, 4737/23 Ansari Road, Daryaganj, New Delhi 110 002.

Printed and bound at Anand Sons, Delhi - 110 092.

Contents

Preface

If it better suits your circumstances, split the test material provided in this book into smaller tests and adjust the recommended time allowed accordingly. Alternatively, remove some of the questions from a test to use for practice free of time constraints.

If you are having difficulty finding practice material relevant to the test that you face then by all means write to me care of Kogan Page, enclosing details of the test and a telephone number or e-mail address, and I will be glad to inform you of any sources that I know.

I apologize in advance for any errors that you find. Try not to let it undermine your belief in the value of practice. I have tried hard to keep out the errors that somehow creep into a text of this kind. I will be glad to hear of any that I have missed, care of Kogan Page, in order that they can be removed at the next reprint.

May I take this opportunity to wish you every success in your career and good luck in the psychometric tests that you face.

Preface

1

Psychometric testing in context

This book contains over 500 realistic practice questions. They have been written to afford valuable practice before taking a graduate psychometric test for real. Use them as part of a programme of revision for managerial or graduate psychometric tests.

Most readers will have applied for a graduate or managerial position or course of study and found that the process involves a test. In this context, psychometric tests are competitions used by the institution or employer for selection purposes. They comprise a standardized series of problems, usually multiple choice or short answer, taken with a pen and paper or increasingly at a computer terminal. The conditions under which the test is taken will be the same for all candidates, and for many tests a strict time limit will apply. They are marked or scored and the results allow comparisons to be drawn between the candidates.

At the graduate and managerial end of the testing spectrum they are likely to comprise a series of sub-tests taken one after the other over a number of hours with only a short pause between papers. There may be many candidates competing for a quite small number of opportunities and under these circumstances you will have to be at your very best if you are to succeed.

Psychometric testing is widespread and many graduate or management positions or courses will require you to undergo some sort of test or series of tests during the selection process. At the graduate level they are likely to be tests of your stamina and endurance and seek to investigate aspects of your interests, personality and abilities.

There are many types of test used at the graduate and management level. Some are specialist to a particular career or profession, others are general. The tests that you face are likely to be a combination of both specialist and general. A non-exhaustive list of types of tests from which your tests will be drawn includes:

- personality questionnaires;
- interest inventories;
- motivational questionnaires;
- verbal analysis;
- numerical analysis;
- work sample and in-tray tests;
- tests of accuracy and fault diagnosis;
- mechanical and technical reasoning;
- abstract and spatial reasoning.

A questionnaire will not normally have a time limit while a test will be strictly timed.

Before you sit a psychometric test or questionnaire you should find out as much as you possibly can about it. The internet is a great source of this kind of information but material should also be available as an information sheet or over the telephone. The organization that has invited you to a test should provide you with, or direct you to, this information.

How you approach a psychometric test is critical to success. Avoid any feelings of resentment or a fear of failure if these feelings mean that you commit less than your full effort. Push negative thoughts aside and decide to treat it as an opportunity to demonstrate your true worth. If passing this test means that you can realize a life goal then you have no alternative but to try your best and attend fully prepared.

If you suffer a disability that will affect your ability to complete any aspect of the selection process then inform the organization immediately.

In many instances you may be allowed extra time to complete the test or they may organize things differently in order to accommodate your needs.

How you score in a test is largely dependent on how well you have prepared for the challenge. Everyone can improve on their test score with practice. But you need to practise a lot if you want to show a significant improvement.

If you really want to do well then you need to set about a programme of preparation. If the position to which you apply is heavily oversubscribed then set about a major programme of practice. Other candidates will be doing this, so do the same or risk coming a poor second. At the graduate management level you may well need to practise for weeks or even months.

You will not be able to get hold of past papers or real copies of the test. You will need far more material than that provided by the organization or test publisher. To prepare properly you will require many hundreds, thousands even, of practice questions. These questions will have to be of the right type and at a suitable level of difficulty.

There are books in the Kogan Page Testing Series that cover most types of real test and questionnaires at both intermediate and advanced levels. You will not find all the material that you need in one title but will need to work from a number from the series. Depending on your starting point, it may be best if you begin with intermediate titles and then progress to the more advanced.

How to make best use of this workbook

This book is intended to help you practise for the three most common parts of graduate or management tests: the personality questionnaires, the numerical analysis sub-tests and the verbal analysis sub-tests. It is intended as a companion to the best-selling title *How to Pass Graduate Psychometric Tests*, also written by me, and by working from both titles you will have over 1,000 questions on which to practise. Other Kogan Page titles will provide further material on which you may practise.

I have included material that will benefit most applicants; however, this may mean that not all the material is relevant to your situation. Seek the most appropriate material in terms of both the level of difficulty and question type. Skip material that you find too easy, or adjust the time allowed to make it more of a challenge. Alternatively, leave material you find hard until a later stage in your programme of practice.

To benefit most you need to undertake two sorts of practice. You should start work in a relaxed situation, with others if possible, without constraint of time, reviewing examples of questions, working out the answers and becoming familiar with the demands. Feel free to review the correct answers and explanations provided at any point during this stage of your programme. Refer to textbooks, dictionaries or a calculator as much as you wish.

Once you are familiar with the challenge you should start to practise under realistic test conditions. This involves putting aside the calculator or dictionary and working against the clock without help or interruption. The aim is to develop a good exam technique and to improve your stamina and endurance. Do not spend too long on questions and stop when you run out of time. After the test you should review the answers and explanations provided and go over your wrong answers to better understand where you made mistakes or to identify gaps in your knowledge that you can then set about resolving.

All the material in this book has been arranged as practice tests with recommended time limits. The practice tests are realistic in terms of the relevance of the questions and the sheer hard work and concentration that are required of candidates for graduate and management psychometric tests. In the companion title *How to Pass Graduate Psychometric Tests* you will find a useful diagnostic exercise and glossary of terms as well as many hundreds of further practice questions.

Set yourself a personal challenge

To get the most out of these practice tests, set yourself the personal challenge of trying to beat your last score each time you take a test. That way you will prove to yourself the value of practice and create a more realistic real test feel.

You need to try really hard and take the challenge seriously if you are to realize this aim.

Proceed by following this 11-step programme:

Step 1. Undertake the familiarization work described above.

Step 2. Take the first test, either analysis of information test 2 or data interpretation test 4.

Step 3. Score that test and review your answers in light of the explanations provided.

Step 4. Read the appropriate interpretation of your score.

Step 5. Undertake more practice, making sure that you address any identified gaps in your knowledge or skills. Obtain this practice material from the companion title or other Kogan Page titles.

Step 6. Set yourself the challenge of beating your first score.

Step 7. Get yourself in the right frame of mind and really 'go for it' in the next practice test.

Step 8. Score it and revise your answers and the interpretation of your second score.

Step 9. Repeat step 5.

Step 10. In the case of data interpretation, take test 6 and again try to get a new personal best score.

Step 11. Calculate your percentage scores in order to make comparisons. Record your scores in the boxes below.

Analysis of information

Percentage scores

Test 2

☐

Test 3

☐

Percentage improvement

☐

Data interpretation

Percentage scores

Test 4

☐

Test 5

☐

Test 6

☐

Percentage improvement (between tests 4 and 6)

☐

Try not to fear failure

It is possible that more candidates will fail than pass a graduate psychometric test or questionnaire. This is especially the case if the position or place is heavily oversubscribed. Many of the candidates lucky enough to pass will have previously failed a test or even previously failed the same test. If you fail, it does not mean that you do not have the potential to do the job or pursue the career. In fact it says very little about you, so try not to take it personally. You may be perfectly able to do the job and indeed you might have passed the test if there had been fewer candidates or if you retook the test having benefited from the first experience.

Ask the organization to provide you with feedback and use this information to identify the areas in which you most need to improve. Recall and make a note of the type of questions and the level of difficulty. Plan a new programme of practice concentrating on the areas in which you did less well. Try again, this time much better informed of the challenge.

Failing should not prejudice any future applications that you make. There may be a rule that means you cannot reapply immediately or for a period afterwards. However, many successful candidates have only passed on their third or fourth attempt and go on to enjoy an unimpeded career within the organization of their choice.

2

Test 1: Graduate personality questionnaire

A personality questionnaire requires you to indicate how you respond to a variety of situations or statements. Such questionnaires comprise many tens of questions and you must indicate whether you agree or disagree with the sentiment expressed. Alternatively, they describe a situation and offer a number of possible responses; it is your task to decide which of the responses is the most appropriate.

The same issue is often explored with more than one question, each phrased differently and approaching the issue from a variety of perspectives (usually widely dispersed through the test). Test authors repeat issues to try to see if you are consistent in your response and they take inconstancy to mean that the applicant may be being disingenuous in their responses.

Most people answer these questionnaires far too quickly and fail to consider the questions sufficiently. The questionnaire is often sent out with the application pack or features early on in the recruitment process, perhaps on a website. If this is true in your case then realize that the questionnaire may be used to reject a large number of applicants. How you present yourself in the questionnaire will determine whether or not you are passed through to the next stage of the recruitment process. Rushing the questionnaire will mean that you fail to give the best impression possible and for many candidates rushing will invite rejection simply because they have failed to take the questionnaire seriously.

Another common error is to answer the question outside of the context in which the question is asked. Constantly remind yourself of the context. You are applying for a particular role; they are trying to identify candidates with suitable personalities for a particular position and organization. Always answer the questions in this context. Avoid the all too common mistake of getting too philosophical about the issue or imagining a non-work situation when you might answer the question differently. See every question from the perspective of the employer. If the questionnaire asks 'Is honesty always the best policy?', realize that the employer is expecting a positive response despite the fact that you can imagine an unlikely and far-fetched scenario where dishonesty might be kinder or in the interest of the person to whom you are lying.

Be prepared to make a response or series of responses that you feel might not support your application. Honesty is the only policy. It is possible that a single 'wrong' response can lead to a rejected application; this can apply to issues that are considered essential to the role, but the vast majority of the questions that make up a questionnaire will not be so critical and every candidate will make a number of low-scoring responses. If the questionnaire asks 'Are you fluent in a second European language?' and you are not, then avoid any temptation to mislead. Questions of competency in particular are very likely to be picked up later in the process or, worse, could land you a job in which you cannot perform.

There is no conflict between giving honest responses and making sure that you present yourself as well as possible. Some features of your character might be judged by an employer as a good quality while another might be put off by those features. It is perfectly reasonable, therefore, that you should stress some parts of your personality over others, depending on your understanding of what the employer wants. All candidates seek to make their application as attractive as possible. Study the information sent to you by the employer, reread the advertisement, find out as much as you can about the culture and preferred working style of the organization. Keep this information in mind when deciding whether or not to agree or agree strongly with a statement. For example, if the advertisement states that the organization is looking for someone who likes to get their teeth into a problem, and you respond well in such a culture, then emphasize that aspect of your personality when deciding your response to the statements contained in the questionnaire. Alternatively, use this information to realize that this is not the sort of establishment that you want to join and look elsewhere.

Try not to overdo the number of responses that suggest you find it difficult to decide; nor should you indicate too many responses as strongly held views.

There is not normally a time limit for the completion of personality questionnaires.

Over the page is a 130-question practice graduate personality questionnaire. Use it to reflect on typical styles of question posed in real tests. Practise being consistent in your answers. Remember that a negative response may be consistent with a previous positive response.

It is not possible to identify a correct response to these questions. How an organization might weight your responses would depend on the role for which you are applying and the organization's priorities and preferred working style. In the chapter Answers and many detailed explanations I have provided an interpretation of the question and identified other questions to which a consistent response might be expected. These comments are intended only to help you develop an effective approach to these common tests. Do not draw from the comments any conclusions regarding your aptitude for any particular role or career. Simply use the questions to familiarize yourself with these very common tests, to realize how an employer is likely to interpret your responses and to help you to decide how to present your personal attributes in the best possible light.

Test 1: Graduate personality questionnaire

Test instructions

This test comprises 130 questions and there is no time limit.

Each question consists of a statement or describes a situation and offers a choice of responses. It is your task to decide your personal response. You should think carefully about the statement or situation and answer the questions honestly.

You should attempt all 130 questions and provide an answer to them all.

The answer you give will depend on your personal circumstances so it is not possible to give correct or incorrect answers. However, an interpretation of each statement is provided on pages 159–170 and other questions are listed which you should consider for consistency of your responses.

To get the most out of the practice test, decide on a position to which you might apply and have in mind a particular organization. Decide on a number of features of your personality that you feel would best represent you for that position and to that organization and try to emphasize those qualities in particular and above others in your responses.

During the test, reflect on the statements and situations carefully, keeping in mind the position to which you are applying and the preferred working style of the organization.

Use this test to practise becoming more consistent in your responses.

1. Sometimes you have to take stock and be sure that all the financial needs and objectives of the organization will be served before you press on with a new initiative.

A Agree strongly
B Agree
C Do not agree or disagree
D Disagree
E Disagree strongly

Answer

2. I can rely on my own initiative.

A Agree strongly
B Agree
C Do not agree or disagree
D Disagree
E Disagree strongly

Answer

3. Others would describe me as unflappable.

A Agree strongly
B Agree
C Do not agree or disagree
D Disagree
E Disagree strongly

Answer

4. I like nothing more than getting my teeth into a challenge.

A Agree strongly
B Agree
C Do not agree or disagree
D Disagree
E Disagree strongly

Answer

5. It pays to plan for the worst case even if it is very unlikely to happen.

A Agree strongly
B Agree
C Do not agree or disagree
D Disagree
E Disagree strongly

Answer

6. Accuracy should not be sacrificed to speed.

A Agree strongly
B Agree
C Do not agree or disagree
D Disagree
E Disagree strongly

Answer

7. I would describe myself as people friendly.

A Agree strongly
B Agree
C Do not agree or disagree
D Disagree
E Disagree strongly

Answer

8. Keeping things simple makes for good business.

A Agree strongly
B Agree
C Do not agree or disagree
D Disagree
E Disagree strongly

Answer

9. I would describe myself as a long-term player.

A Agree strongly
B Agree
C Do not agree or disagree
D Disagree
E Disagree strongly

Answer

10. My career to date owes much to my exceptional people skills.

A Agree strongly
B Agree
C Do not agree or disagree
D Disagree
E Disagree strongly

Answer

11. Drive and determination alone will effect a positive solution to most challenges.

A Agree strongly
B Agree
C Do not agree or disagree
D Disagree
E Disagree strongly

Answer

12. In the real world, leadership is more about leading people through unforeseen challenges than being able to visualize, communicate and deploy strategies.

A Agree strongly
B Agree
C Do not agree or disagree
D Disagree
E Disagree strongly

Answer

13. I am an exceptional relationship builder.

A Agree strongly
B Agree
C Do not agree or disagree
D Disagree
E Disagree strongly

Answer

14. I have an exemplary written style.

A Agree strongly
B Agree
C Do not agree or disagree
D Disagree
E Disagree strongly

Answer

15. Whatever my role I am determined to make a difference.

A Agree strongly
B Agree
C Do not agree or disagree
D Disagree
E Disagree strongly

☐ Answer

16. I never tire of new tools, technologies or ideas.

A Agree strongly
B Agree
C Do not agree or disagree
D Disagree
E Disagree strongly

☐ Answer

17. I prefer realistic, down to earth solutions.

A Agree strongly
B Agree
C Do not agree or disagree
D Disagree
E Disagree strongly

☐ Answer

18. I find intolerance inexcusable.

A Agree strongly
B Agree
C Do not agree or disagree
D Disagree
E Disagree strongly

☐ Answer

19. I like to have every eventuality covered.

A Agree strongly
B Agree
C Do not agree or disagree
D Disagree
E Disagree strongly

Answer

20. One of my strengths is data analysis.

A Agree strongly
B Agree
C Do not agree or disagree
D Disagree
E Disagree strongly

Answer

21. I set myself deadlines and I adhere to them.

A Agree strongly
B Agree
C Do not agree or disagree
D Disagree
E Disagree strongly

Answer

22. Others regard me as totally reliable and I really do hate letting others down.

A Agree strongly
B Agree
C Do not agree or disagree
D Disagree
E Disagree strongly

Answer

23. Key to my management approach is the ability to enthuse others.

A Agree strongly
B Agree
C Do not agree or disagree
D Disagree
E Disagree strongly

[ ] Answer

24. I would not hesitate to ring a colleague at the weekend to establish how an important issue was resolved.

A Agree strongly
B Agree
C Do not agree or disagree
D Disagree
E Disagree strongly

[ ] Answer

25. For an organization to stay competitive you have to constantly challenge the status quo.

A Agree strongly
B Agree
C Do not agree or disagree
D Disagree
E Disagree strongly

[ ] Answer

26. I will travel by bus, train, car or plane to see the deal done.

A Agree strongly
B Agree
C Do not agree or disagree
D Disagree
E Disagree strongly

Answer

27. I excel in a role that demands strategic awareness.

A Agree strongly
B Agree
C Do not agree or disagree
D Disagree
E Disagree strongly

Answer

28. Above all else, others would describe me as dependable.

A Agree strongly
B Agree
C Do not agree or disagree
D Disagree
E Disagree strongly

Answer

29. I am happiest working in a no-blame culture.

A Agree strongly
B Agree
C Do not agree or disagree
D Disagree
E Disagree strongly

Answer

30. I feel uncomfortable if I am anything less than autonomous.

A Agree strongly
B Agree
C Do not agree or disagree
D Disagree
E Disagree strongly

Answer

31. Always find the time to predict the next challenge even if it distracts you from the most immediate threat.

A Agree strongly
B Agree
C Do not agree or disagree
D Disagree
E Disagree strongly

Answer

32. A balanced sense of humour is an asset in any workplace.

A Agree strongly
B Agree
C Do not agree or disagree
D Disagree
E Disagree strongly

Answer

33. I am uncomfortable with ambiguity.

A Agree strongly
B Agree
C Do not agree or disagree
D Disagree
E Disagree strongly

Answer

34. Only if I am qualified in a subject area do I feel well placed to contribute to a debate.

A Agree strongly
B Agree
C Do not agree or disagree
D Disagree
E Disagree strongly

Answer

35. More than anything I want to influence.

A Agree strongly
B Agree
C Do not agree or disagree
D Disagree
E Disagree strongly

Answer

36. The devil is in the detail.

A Agree strongly
B Agree
C Do not agree or disagree
D Disagree
E Disagree strongly

Answer

37. I work best if I have an agreed set of performance indicators against which my contribution can be judged.

A Agree strongly
B Agree
C Do not agree or disagree
D Disagree
E Disagree strongly

Answer

38. I take great pride in my impartiality.

A Agree strongly
B Agree
C Do not agree or disagree
D Disagree
E Disagree strongly

Answer

39. I like responsibility.

A Agree strongly
B Agree
C Do not agree or disagree
D Disagree
E Disagree strongly

Answer

40. I am naturally averse to risk.

A Agree strongly
B Agree
C Do not agree or disagree
D Disagree
E Disagree strongly

Answer

41. I pride myself on demonstrating exemplary management skills.

A Agree strongly
B Agree
C Do not agree or disagree
D Disagree
E Disagree strongly

Answer

42. I believe passionately that an empowering approach to management gets the most out of a team.

A Agree strongly
B Agree
C Do not agree or disagree
D Disagree
E Disagree strongly

Answer

43. It is not my job to change a light bulb.

A Agree strongly
B Agree
C Do not agree or disagree
D Disagree
E Disagree strongly

Answer

44. Change is best achieved step by step.

A Agree strongly
B Agree
C Do not agree or disagree
D Disagree
E Disagree strongly

Answer

45. A problem anticipated is a problem halved.

A Agree strongly
B Agree
C Do not agree or disagree
D Disagree
E Disagree strongly

Answer

46. I pride myself on being able to pick up on the big issues very quickly.

A Agree strongly
B Agree
C Do not agree or disagree
D Disagree
E Disagree strongly

Answer

47. It is important to me that I stand out as an individual.

A Agree strongly
B Agree
C Do not agree or disagree
D Disagree
E Disagree strongly

Answer

48. An important part of my role at work is to provide counsel.

A Agree strongly
B Agree
C Do not agree or disagree
D Disagree
E Disagree strongly

Answer

49. If you cannot provide inspiration then you risk failing to bring others fully along with you.

A Agree strongly
B Agree
C Do not agree or disagree
D Disagree
E Disagree strongly

Answer

50. I do not have time to look at them all but I like to be copied into every e-mail.

A Agree strongly
B Agree
C Do not agree or disagree
D Disagree
E Disagree strongly

Answer

51. Others describe me as an able communicator.

A Agree strongly
B Agree
C Do not agree or disagree
D Disagree
E Disagree strongly

Answer

52. A compromise is rarely good for business.

    A Agree strongly
    B Agree
    C Do not agree or disagree
    D Disagree
    E Disagree strongly

    ☐ Answer

53. I bring natural stature to a role.

    A Agree strongly
    B Agree
    C Do not agree or disagree
    D Disagree
    E Disagree strongly

    ☐ Answer

54. The only way to approach ambiguity is with a good dose of clarity of thought.

    A Agree strongly
    B Agree
    C Do not agree or disagree
    D Disagree
    E Disagree strongly

    ☐ Answer

55. I pride myself on being able to recognize an opportunity.

    A Agree strongly
    B Agree
    C Do not agree or disagree
    D Disagree
    E Disagree strongly

    ☐ Answer

56. My colleagues will confirm that I can be very persuasive.

A Agree strongly
B Agree
C Do not agree or disagree
D Disagree
E Disagree strongly

☐ Answer

57. It is very important to me to be judged competent in my role.

A Agree strongly
B Agree
C Do not agree or disagree
D Disagree
E Disagree strongly

☐ Answer

58. I want to see incredible earning power from day one.

A Agree strongly
B Agree
C Do not agree or disagree
D Disagree
E Disagree strongly

☐ Answer

59. If people applied a bit more common sense then half the problems that occur at work would be avoided.

A Agree strongly
B Agree
C Do not agree or disagree
D Disagree
E Disagree strongly

☐ Answer

60. I demand very high standards of work from myself and others.

A Agree strongly
B Agree
C Do not agree or disagree
D Disagree
E Disagree strongly

☐ Answer

61. Integrity cannot be compromised.

A Agree strongly
B Agree
C Do not agree or disagree
D Disagree
E Disagree strongly

☐ Answer

62. Loss prevention or reduction is more important than fee earning.

A Agree strongly
B Agree
C Do not agree or disagree
D Disagree
E Disagree strongly

☐ Answer

63. I prefer to organize and prioritize my own work.

A Agree strongly
B Agree
C Do not agree or disagree
D Disagree
E Disagree strongly

☐ Answer

64. In business you need fast reflexes.

A Agree strongly
B Agree
C Do not agree or disagree
D Disagree
E Disagree strongly

Answer

65. Being matter-of-fact is very positive.

A Agree strongly
B Agree
C Do not agree or disagree
D Disagree
E Disagree strongly

Answer

66. I am decisive within my area of knowledge.

A Agree strongly
B Agree
C Do not agree or disagree
D Disagree
E Disagree strongly

Answer

67. I get a great deal of job satisfaction as a result of being able to streamline processes.

A Agree strongly
B Agree
C Do not agree or disagree
D Disagree
E Disagree strongly

Answer

68. Regulation stifles invention and creativity.

A Agree strongly
B Agree
C Do not agree or disagree
D Disagree
E Disagree strongly

Answer

69. I make my contribution on the right-hand side of the balance sheet.

A Agree strongly
B Agree
C Do not agree or disagree
D Disagree
E Disagree strongly

Answer

70. Sometimes you have to tell people to stop talking and listen for a change.

A Agree strongly
B Agree
C Do not agree or disagree
D Disagree
E Disagree strongly

Answer

71. It is true that the higher the return the higher the risk.

A Agree strongly
B Agree
C Do not agree or disagree
D Disagree
E Disagree strongly

Answer

72. I relish a broad workload.

A Agree strongly
B Agree
C Do not agree or disagree
D Disagree
E Disagree strongly

Answer

73. Every business can benefit from a few regulations and written procedures.

A Agree strongly
B Agree
C Do not agree or disagree
D Disagree
E Disagree strongly

Answer

74. I am highly self-disciplined.

A Agree strongly
B Agree
C Do not agree or disagree
D Disagree
E Disagree strongly

Answer

75. My approach is simple – it involves identifying the source of the problem and generating solutions quickly.

A Agree strongly
B Agree
C Do not agree or disagree
D Disagree
E Disagree strongly

Answer

76. Being unbiased is very important to me.

A Agree strongly
B Agree
C Do not agree or disagree
D Disagree
E Disagree strongly

Answer

77. I work best when I am allowed to get on with the job and distractions are kept to a minimum.

A Agree strongly
B Agree
C Do not agree or disagree
D Disagree
E Disagree strongly

Answer

78. A consistent approach at work is far better than one that relies on inspired bursts of energy.

A Agree strongly
B Agree
C Do not agree or disagree
D Disagree
E Disagree strongly

Answer

79. I would describe my current role as multitasked.

A Agree strongly
B Agree
C Do not agree or disagree
D Disagree
E Disagree strongly

Answer

80. Knowledge is power and is a commodity like any other so I prefer to keep it to myself.

A Agree strongly
B Agree
C Do not agree or disagree
D Disagree
E Disagree strongly

Answer

81. Work is about where I am going, not where I am from.

A Agree strongly
B Agree
C Do not agree or disagree
D Disagree
E Disagree strongly

Answer

82. My success is down to my strong interpersonal skills.

A Agree strongly
B Agree
C Do not agree or disagree
D Disagree
E Disagree strongly

Answer

83. I am highly focused on solving problems.

A Agree strongly
B Agree
C Do not agree or disagree
D Disagree
E Disagree strongly

Answer

84. When something goes wrong it is best to put it right and then report it.

A Agree strongly
B Agree
C Do not agree or disagree
D Disagree
E Disagree strongly

Answer

85. Others regard me as meticulous.

A Agree strongly
B Agree
C Do not agree or disagree
D Disagree
E Disagree strongly

Answer

86. At work it is best not to upset people by telling them something they do not want to hear.

A Agree strongly
B Agree
C Do not agree or disagree
D Disagree
E Disagree strongly

Answer

87. My drive and determination are the keys to my success.

A Agree strongly
B Agree
C Do not agree or disagree
D Disagree
E Disagree strongly

Answer

88. I am highly flexible in my approach.

A Agree strongly
B Agree
C Do not agree or disagree
D Disagree
E Disagree strongly

Answer

89. Like organic things, a business must be moved towards warmth and away from pain.

A Agree strongly
B Agree
C Do not agree or disagree
D Disagree
E Disagree strongly

Answer

90. Above all else, others would describe me as goal orientated.

A Agree strongly
B Agree
C Do not agree or disagree
D Disagree
E Disagree strongly

Answer

91. I absolutely refuse to be browbeaten.

A Agree strongly
B Agree
C Do not agree or disagree
D Disagree
E Disagree strongly

Answer

92. I despair that in this day and age of targets and measurement there is no credit given to all the outcomes that you can't put numbers on.

A Agree strongly
B Agree
C Do not agree or disagree
D Disagree
E Disagree strongly

Answer

93. I have a very direct approach.

A Agree strongly
B Agree
C Do not agree or disagree
D Disagree
E Disagree strongly

Answer

94. I have to be able to appreciate the bigger picture.

A Agree strongly
B Agree
C Do not agree or disagree
D Disagree
E Disagree strongly

Answer

95. I prefer to give orders rather than receive them.

A Agree strongly
B Agree
C Do not agree or disagree
D Disagree
E Disagree strongly

Answer

96. I must get involved in the detail if I am to manage others well.

A Agree strongly
B Agree
C Do not agree or disagree
D Disagree
E Disagree strongly

Answer

97. I am happy to muck in.

A Agree strongly
B Agree
C Do not agree or disagree
D Disagree
E Disagree strongly

Answer

98. When problems arrive I deal with them.

A Agree strongly
B Agree
C Do not agree or disagree
D Disagree
E Disagree strongly

Answer

99. I would describe myself as polished.

A Agree strongly
B Agree
C Do not agree or disagree
D Disagree
E Disagree strongly

Answer

100. Prudence is undervalued in many organizations.

A Agree strongly
B Agree
C Do not agree or disagree
D Disagree
E Disagree strongly

Answer

101. I have a genuine talent for establishing new leads.

A Agree strongly
B Agree
C Do not agree or disagree
D Disagree
E Disagree strongly

Answer

102. I pride myself on being able to do the job while dealing sensitively with people and issues.

A Agree strongly
B Agree
C Do not agree or disagree
D Disagree
E Disagree strongly

Answer

103. I have a proven aptitude for business development.

A Agree strongly
B Agree
C Do not agree or disagree
D Disagree
E Disagree strongly

Answer

104. There is no more rewarding challenge than rebuilding a ship plank by plank while remaining afloat.

A Agree strongly
B Agree
C Do not agree or disagree
D Disagree
E Disagree strongly

Answer

105. The only way to bring about change for the better is to drive it through personally, step by step.

A Agree strongly
B Agree
C Do not agree or disagree
D Disagree
E Disagree strongly

Answer

106. If a colleague did not find me dynamic then I would be failing in my role.

A Agree strongly
B Agree
C Do not agree or disagree
D Disagree
E Disagree strongly

Answer

107. I operate a no-blame culture.

A Agree strongly
B Agree
C Do not agree or disagree
D Disagree
E Disagree strongly

Answer

108. You can never know it all and should always be prepared to adopt new ways of working.

A Agree strongly
B Agree
C Do not agree or disagree
D Disagree
E Disagree strongly

Answer

109. I understand the importance to staff morale of demonstrating effective listening skills.

A Agree strongly
B Agree
C Do not agree or disagree
D Disagree
E Disagree strongly

Answer

110. I excel in a client-facing role.

A Agree strongly
B Agree
C Do not agree or disagree
D Disagree
E Disagree strongly

Answer

111. I am 100 per cent customer focused; the rest can look after itself.

A Agree strongly
B Agree
C Do not agree or disagree
D Disagree
E Disagree strongly

Answer

112. I count as one of my achievements in life the fact that I have succeeded in raising funds for a new high-profile venture.

A Agree strongly
B Agree
C Do not agree or disagree
D Disagree
E Disagree strongly

Answer

113. I feel happiest when I can implement defined regulatory processes.

A Agree strongly
B Agree
C Do not agree or disagree
D Disagree
E Disagree strongly

Answer

114. My colleagues would describe me as entirely open to new ways of working.

A Agree strongly
B Agree
C Do not agree or disagree
D Disagree
E Disagree strongly

Answer

115. I can bring considerable experience of the field to my next position.

A Agree strongly
B Agree
C Do not agree or disagree
D Disagree
E Disagree strongly

Answer

116. I am only too happy to share knowledge with my colleagues.

A Agree strongly
B Agree
C Do not agree or disagree
D Disagree
E Disagree strongly

Answer

117. I want to be a star and I am prepared to work incredibly hard in order to be one.

A Agree strongly
B Agree
C Do not agree or disagree
D Disagree
E Disagree strongly

☐ Answer

118. Eventually, common sense prevails.

A Agree strongly
B Agree
C Do not agree or disagree
D Disagree
E Disagree strongly

☐ Answer

119. It is everyone's right to make mistakes. I only ask of them that they tell me about it straight away.

A Agree strongly
B Agree
C Do not agree or disagree
D Disagree
E Disagree strongly

☐ Answer

120. Success does not come to you; you go to it with self-confidence and a strong need for control and independence.

A Agree strongly
B Agree
C Do not agree or disagree
D Disagree
E Disagree strongly

Answer

121. Only gregarious people can succeed in my field.

A Agree strongly
B Agree
C Do not agree or disagree
D Disagree
E Disagree strongly

Answer

122. I am naturally diplomatic.

A Agree strongly
B Agree
C Do not agree or disagree
D Disagree
E Disagree strongly

Answer

123. To take exception is rarely good for business; this does not mean that you have to accept everything, just that there are other ways of getting things sorted.

A Agree strongly
B Agree
C Do not agree or disagree
D Disagree
E Disagree strongly

Answer

124. I have done it before and I am still hungry enough to do it all over again.

A Agree strongly
B Agree
C Do not agree or disagree
D Disagree
E Disagree strongly

Answer

125. There is a bit of me that demands I must be better than the rest.

A Agree strongly
B Agree
C Do not agree or disagree
D Disagree
E Disagree strongly

Answer

126. If you can get people to buy into a set of objectives or targets then everyone will work that bit harder towards a shared goal.

A Agree strongly
B Agree
C Do not agree or disagree
D Disagree
E Disagree strongly

Answer

127. If I can get through the door then I can close the deal.

A Agree strongly
B Agree
C Do not agree or disagree
D Disagree
E Disagree strongly

Answer

128. Being personable can make up for many potential shortfalls.

A Agree strongly
B Agree
C Do not agree or disagree
D Disagree
E Disagree strongly

Answer

129. Success demands a high degree of boldness.

A Agree strongly
B Agree
C Do not agree or disagree
D Disagree
E Disagree strongly

Answer

130. I would describe myself as reasonable, competent, measured and considered.

A Agree strongly
B Agree
C Do not agree or disagree
D Disagree
E Disagree strongly

Answer

End of the questionnaire

3

Tests 2 and 3: Analysis of information

This chapter contains 133 questions organized between two practice tests. You are presented with a series of short passages each followed by three or sometimes four statements or questions. Your task is to indicate whether the statement or question is true, false or you cannot tell.

You answer these questions with reference only to the content of the passage and what can be inferred from it. With this type of question you sometimes find yourself saying something is true or false that you know not to be the case or confirming as true or false something with which you do not personally agree. This is because you rely only on the content of the passage to answer the questions. Be especially careful if you know lots about the subject covered by a passage as you are then more likely to involve your personal knowledge or opinions and as a result risk getting the question wrong!

In the real tests you have very little time to read the passage and answer the questions. Do not make the mistake of not practising if you find these questions easy when you are free of the pressure of time. In the real test you will only have time for one careful reading. You will have to switch really fast between vastly different subject matter with each passage and keep up a very high level of concentration right to the end. This all takes practice to get really good at.

This question type has become very popular in recent years and features in many graduate and management psychometric tests. With practice you can show a considerable improvement in your score.

Your studies will have already served as good preparation for this type of question, so these practice tests include some that are difficult. To help you develop your exam technique more time has been allowed for the first test.

Answers and explanations are provided on pages 170–186.

An interpretation of your score is provided on pages 209–211.

Test 2: Analysis of information

Test instructions

This test comprises 22 passages and 67 questions.

You are allowed 55 minutes to complete it (that is approximately 50 seconds a question).

You are given a series of passages each of which is followed by a number of statements. It is your task to say whether the statement is true or false or whether it is not possible to say whether the statement is true or false. You should base your decision only on the information or opinions given in the passage.

You should judge the statement to be true only if, for example, it follows logically from the passage or is a rewording of something contained in the passage or is a valid summary of the passage or a part of it.

You should judge the statement to be false if, for example, it cannot follow logically from the passage or if it contradicts something contained in the passage.

If you require more information than is contained in the passage before you can tell if the statement is true or false then you should record your answer as 'cannot tell'.

You should work quickly and not spend too long on any one question.

Work without interruption.

Do not turn over the page until you are ready to begin.

Passage 1

Oil price instability justifies greater efforts to develop substitute fuels. But this should be a part of a two-pronged strategy, the other prong being to make existing fuels go further. Regrettably, however, the effort is still not there. Heat loss in homes and factories represents a substantial and avoidable waste. In transport, petrol is used relatively efficiently but it could be used to go even further still.

1. Not enough is being done to make better use of fuels.

   A True
   B False
   C Cannot tell

   Answer

2. The opportunity to make existing fuels go further exists mainly in the domestic sector.

   A True
   B False
   C Cannot tell

   Answer

3. Oil price instability will lead to greater efforts to use existing fuel sources more efficiently.

   A True
   B False
   C Cannot tell

   Answer

Passage 2

The New Homes Group delivered its half-year results with profits up by 50% and turnover and average selling price all strongly ahead. This was a record performance for the group and relates to a period when the housing market was rising sharply. Since then the market has dipped following a succession of interest rate rises and a drop in consumer confidence.

4. The next half-year results may not be so impressive.

   A True
   B False
   C Cannot tell

   ☐ Answer

5. During this period New Homes were selling properties at 50% higher prices.

   A True
   B False
   C Cannot tell

   ☐ Answer

6. House buyers remain just as optimistic.

   A True
   B False
   C Cannot tell

   ☐ Answer

Passage 3

It is estimated that one in four children aged between 4 and 11 contract head lice each year. Children in urban schools are particularly prone. Girls and boys are infected by a ratio of three to one. This is related to the fact that girls' play tends to involve more prolonged contact between heads. Head lice live close to the scalp and feed on blood. The itch they cause is from the bite made when they are feeding. A louse lives for about 300 days and a female will lay over 2,000 eggs in her lifetime.

7. Boys aged between 4 and 11 years who go to urban schools are more likely to contact head lice than girls.

   A True
   B False
   C Cannot tell

   Answer

8. The length of hair and the frequency with which it is washed are irrelevant to the likelihood of contracting head lice.

   A True
   B False
   C Cannot tell

   Answer

9. A child can contract head lice when prolonged contact between heads occurs.

   A True
   B False
   C Cannot tell

   Answer

Passage 4

Life has been short for the one- and two-cent euro coins launched only three years ago. Faced with chronic shortages, the central banks of Denmark and Belgium have decided they have no alternative but to withdraw them and order retailers to round prices up or down to the nearest five cents, depending which is closest. The French have no such plans; they fear that the rounding of prices might lead to an overall increase in price levels.

10. If there were not such a chronic shortage of the coins the Danish and Belgian central banks would not be withdrawing them.

    A True
    B False
    C Cannot tell

    Answer

11. The shortage of these coins in France is less chronic.

    A True
    B False
    C Cannot tell

    Answer

12. The five-cent coin will shortly be the lowest-value euro coin in circulation.

    A True
    B False
    C Cannot tell

    Answer

Passage 5

For a decade the objective has been the ending of rough sleeping in Britain. New York's tough homelessness policies were adopted and they have been far more effective in London than in New York. Rough sleeping is becoming much rarer in London, while the number of homeless in New York remains high. There are several reasons. The benefits system in the UK is fairly generous when compared to the US system. The hostel accommodation in London has been greatly improved, with dormitories converted to single rooms, making the alternatives to living on the street more attractive than in New York.

13. Improvements to hostel accommodation have made this alternative to rough sleeping more attractive in London than in New York.

    A True
    B False
    C Cannot tell

    Answer

14. Homelessness in Britain has declined.

    A True
    B False
    C Cannot tell

    Answer

15. A justification for a comparison of the occurrence of homelessness between the two cities is made in the passage.

    A True
    B False
    C Cannot tell

    Answer

Passage 6

Traffic levels have fallen by 15% and congestion is down by a third. In August the Mayor of London announced a plan to extend the £5 charge for driving in central London during the working week westwards to Kensington and Chelsea. This was despite a consultative process in which almost 70,000 people and the vast majority of respondents said they did not want the scheme extended. However, the problem with the proposed extension is not only political. Extending the zone to a thickly populated area of London will mean that many people will qualify for the residents' discount, allowing them to drive to the city without paying any extra. Extending the scheme therefore may mean that total revenues drop from the current £90 million a year.

16. The extended scheme may face continued public opposition.

    A True
    B False
    C Cannot tell

    ☐ Answer

17. Kensington and Chelsea have high residential populations.

    A True
    B False
    C Cannot tell

    ☐ Answer

18. People who live in Kensington currently do not have to pay £5 to drive to the city.

    A True
    B False
    C Cannot tell

    ☐ Answer

19. Whilst the majority of respondents voted against the extension it is possible that they welcomed the fall in traffic levels and lower congestion.

A True
B False
C Cannot tell

Answer

Passage 7

The cost of stamp duty for the average house purchase has more than doubled since 1997. In some towns the bills have risen by more than £10,000. Four successive rises in the tax on house purchases and the introduction of incremental bands, with the highest a 4% band for homes valued over £500,000, have sharply increased the amount raised by the Treasury. A spokesperson for the Treasury said that stamp duty remains a very small proportion of overall housing costs and property transaction costs are far lower in the UK than the rest of the EU and United States.

20. Taxation on property transactions in the UK has been increased four times.

A True
B False
C Cannot tell

Answer

21. In some towns the cost of stamp duty on a house purchased in 1997 was less than £5,000.

A True
B False
C Cannot tell

Answer

22. A house sold for half a million pounds incurs a £20,000 stamp duty bill.

A True
B False
C Cannot tell

Answer

Passage 8

A swarm of locusts is a disaster and last month hundreds of swarms were reported in Senegal, Mali, Niger and Chad and vast areas of crops have been destroyed. A locust eats its own weight (2 grams) every day and a swarm contains billions of insects. The swarm can travel 60 miles a day and leave behind it a wasteland stripped of everything green and sown with eggs which hatch after 30 days. The last big locust plague in 1987–88 cost $300 million to stop and the countries affected this year are too poor to cope, so the United Nations has appealed for donors and released $15 million to assist eradication programmes. The most effective method is to spray pesticide from the air or from vehicles. Environmentally friendly methods are more costly and far less effective.

23. The current plague of locusts will cost more than $300 million to stop.

A True
B False
C Cannot tell

Answer

24. The passage states that donors have been asked to provide $15 million in assistance.

A True
B False
C Cannot tell

Answer

25. The next generation of locusts is due to hatch.

A True
B False
C Cannot tell

Answer

Passage 9

Spanish-speaking Americans (Latinos) have overtaken African-Americans as the largest ethnic minority in the United States. The Latino population is growing at over 3% a year, compared with 0.6% for the rest of the population. They are getting richer, accounting for 8% of America's GDP, and are expected to account for 10% of the GDP by 2010. The Latino population is highly concentrated geographically, with two-thirds living in seven states, and they are the youngest population group. Some 75% are of Mexican origin and they want to keep their Mexican culture as well as adopt American values.

26. The passage's opening statement lacks a factual base.

A True
B False
C Cannot tell

Answer

27. It can be inferred from the passage that the Spanish language is the most widely spoken minority language in the United States.

A True
B False
C Cannot tell

Answer

28. The Latino population will comprise 1 in 10 of the American population by 2010.

    A True
    B False
    C Cannot tell

    Answer

Passage 10

Singapore was the first Asian economy to boom and it is booming once again. In the second quarter of this year its economy was 12.5% higher than in the same period the previous year and its government is forecasting future growth at 9% per annum. Some of this growth is due to the passing of the SARS crisis but most was down to a 50% increase in pharmaceutical exports. Most of the world's leading firms now make products in Singapore and its government plans to generate 12 billion a year from this sector by 2010. If this happens, Singapore will avoid recession as jobs in electronics move to China and other low-cost Asian economies.

29. Singapore's first boom was founded on the export of electronics.

    A True
    B False
    C Cannot tell

    Answer

30. This impressive growth is due to an incredible increase in pharmaceutical exports.

    A True
    B False
    C Cannot tell

    Answer

31. Singapore's economy has grown 12.5% in a year.

A True
B False
C Cannot tell

Answer

Passage 11

The world's population is growing by about 70 million people a year but the increase is uneven, with some nations' populations growing rapidly and others decreasing. Among the industrialized nations, only the United States will experience significant growth by 2050, while Europe is expected to have 60 million fewer people than today. Britain is predicted to grow faster than any other European industrialized country, reaching a population of 65 million in the next 25 years. By then it will have overtaken France to become Europe's second most populous country.

32. In all but one case the nations due to experience significant growth in their populations are not industrial.

A True
B False
C Cannot tell

Answer

33. Britain is not expected to experience significant population growth by 2050.

A True
B False
C Cannot tell

Answer

34. Britain is currently the third most populous European country.

A True
B False
C Cannot tell

Answer

Passage 12

The radio audience measurement society is considering whether its quarterly figures for audience numbers should be released earlier to all radio companies but it is concerned to avoid share-price-sensitive information being leaked to the markets. The current situation involves the commercial stations receiving the results 12 hours later than the public channels. A number of commercial stations have questioned this practice, arguing that they too would like to receive the information earlier so that they could prepare press releases before the markets open. The issue has become significant because the commercial stations' share prices tend to move sharply in the hours before the figures are released.

35. An alternative proposal would involve neither type of organization receiving the information early.

A True
B False
C Cannot tell

Answer

36. The commercial stations' share price will go down if the figures show a fall in audience numbers.

A True
B False
C Cannot tell

Answer

37. The passage author fails to present a case for the status quo.

A True
B False
C Cannot tell

☐ Answer

Passage 13

Fifty millimetres of rain across one square kilometre adds up to 50,000 tonnes of water. Such downpours are not rare and on their own they need not cause any significant problem. But if they occur in the wrong place they can cause flash floods, which can be devastating, especially in steep-sided valleys where the torrent can move at tremendous speeds and build up massive momentum. When moving down a steep valley, 15 centimetres of water will sweep a person off their feet; half a metre of water will carry away a car. If water builds up behind debris it can suddenly burst through, creating a wall of water metres high and travelling at speeds up to 45 kilometres per hour.

38. Flash floods occur when heavy rain falls over particular geographic features.

A True
B False
C Cannot tell

☐ Answer

39. A downpour of 15 centimetres of rain is rare.

A True
B False
C Cannot tell

☐ Answer

40. Where a flash flood might occur would be very difficult or impossible even to predict.

A True
B False
C Cannot tell

Answer

Passage 14

Demand for mobile phones in underdeveloped markets such as China and India is leading to ever-higher predictions for global sales. This year analysts have raised their forecasts for the third time to 640 million handsets. This is almost 100 million higher than forecast at the beginning of the year. Some are already forecasting that over 700 million handsets will be sold next year, with analysts convinced that record demand will continue in both developing and mature markets. Only five years ago, total sales were at a global level of 200 million.

41. Next year's predicted record sales are attributed to continued growth in newer markets.

A True
B False
C Cannot tell

Answer

42. Forecast global sales stand 500 million handsets higher than actual sales five years ago.

A True
B False
C Cannot tell

Answer

43. The most recent increase in this year's forecast for sales was almost 100 million handsets higher than the previous forecast.

A True
B False
C Cannot tell

Answer

Passage 15

Scientists have ambitious plans to use cloning technology to save India's lion population from extinction. They believe that biotechnological intervention is a viable modern way to save threatened species. But conservationists argue that the high cost of such experiments would be better spent on protecting animals in their natural habitat. They argue that forests are still being lost to land clearance and India does not have enough wild space left in which the lions can live and hunt.

44. There are many sceptics of the scientists' plans.

A True
B False
C Cannot tell

Answer

45. The passage fails to present the counter-argument.

A True
B False
C Cannot tell

Answer

46. The passage states that the application of biotechnological interventions may have a role in a programme to save the Indian lion from extinction.

A True
B False
C Cannot tell

Answer

Passage 16

A company planning to outsource administrative jobs and its customers' details is being challenged. One of its customers has asked the government-appointed information commissioner to rule on whether or not his personnel files can be legally transferred. The customer believes that the move breaks the Data Protection Act and European legislation that does not allow personal details to be sent outside the European Union without the individual's written consent. If the challenge is successful, the company fears that it may have to abandon its offshore policy.

47. The company plans to transfer personal details and jobs to a company outside of the European Union.

A True
B False
C Cannot tell

Answer

48. There is a conflict between the outsourcing of jobs to non-EU countries and national and European legislation.

A True
B False
C Cannot tell

Answer

49. If the legal challenge were to succeed, an alternative to abandoning the policy might be to obtain the written consent of all the company's customers to the transfer.

A True
B False
C Cannot tell

Answer

Passage 17

Twenty-four billion is invested in premium bonds and in the past 10 years the number of bonds in the draw has increased sevenfold. The chances of winning have recently changed from 27,500 to one to 24,000 to one. Record sales have meant that a new machine to select winning numbers randomly was required. The predecessor took five and a half hours to complete the draw, while the new machine can complete the task in half that time. Each month there are 1 million winners.

50. The chances of winning a prize have increased and there are now more winners' numbers.

A True
B False
C Cannot tell

Answer

51. The new machine takes 150 minutes to draw the 1 million winning numbers.

A True
B False
C Cannot tell

Answer

52. The new machine is a computer.

A True
B False
C Cannot tell

Answer

Passage 18

The government wants 50 per cent of people aged 18 to 30 to go to university, and many of these new students are expected to study for shorter foundation degrees. These last two years and combine study with hands-on experience while in paid relevant work. Already more than 20,000 people are taking foundation degrees in 1,000 different courses. Self-discipline and strong motivation are critical if the student is to succeed because most foundation degrees are by distance learning and are part-time. While foundation degrees are not for the faint-hearted, they may appeal to many students who currently follow conventional university courses and who leave university with average debts of £30,000 and then have to compete for a graduate-level job against other foundation degree graduates with work-related experience.

53. It can be inferred from the passage that part-time study by distant learning demands a higher level of self-discipline than shown by students on conventional degree courses.

A True
B False
C Cannot tell

Answer

54. To undertake a foundation degree does not require one to go to university.

A True
B False
C Cannot tell

Answer

55. The case made for doing a foundation degree rather than a conventional degree is purely economic.

A True
B False
C Cannot tell

Answer

Passage 19

Manufacturing around the globe is being hit by strong increases in the cost of commodities. In some industries, such as the automotive sector, it is common that contracts require annual price reductions. This means that manufacturers in these sectors are unable to pass on price increases. In other sectors there seems to be a general acceptance that prices are having to go up. Manufacturers in some parts of the world also face pressure from emission trading and climate change legislation.

56. You can infer from the passage that some automotive manufacturers will have to cease trading.

A True
B False
C Cannot tell

Answer

57. You would expect the immediate effect of this price pressure to be the erosion of margins.

A True
B False
C Cannot tell

Answer

58. The passage implies that commodity price inflation is the most serious threat to manufacturers.

A True
B False
C Cannot tell

Answer

Passage 20

Labour worldwide is far less mobile than capital. However, this does not mean that governments can ignore the needs of enterprise or investors. A hundred years ago, mass migration across the Atlantic fuelled the growth of the American economy. Migrants took factory jobs at lower wages. In this day and age, factories are more likely to migrate than workers, mainly because of national barriers against immigration. In such a globalized world, governments must ensure that their economies remain internationally competitive.

59. Labour is less mobile than a century ago.

A True
B False
C Cannot tell

Answer

60. Barriers against immigration mean that governments must ensure that their economies remain internationally competitive.

A True
B False
C Cannot tell

Answer

61. The passage suggests that the world would be less globalized if labour were free to move.

A True
B False
C Cannot tell

Answer

Passage 21

Government, politicians and the media perpetuate prejudice and inequality by repeating the lie that teenage mothers place irresponsible burdens on the state. Public service employers should question their approach to teenage women and accept that they have as much right to make choices about pregnancy and motherhood as everyone else. Society should confront the causes of teenage pregnancy, such as inadequate education and employment opportunities, not the women themselves. Teenage mothers need our support and at least equal treatment, and recognition that a young mother is not necessarily a bad mother.

62. Portraying teenage mothers as social problems is discriminatory.

A True
B False
C Cannot tell

Answer

63. The passage describes negative stereotypes of young mothers as prevalent.

A True
B False
C Cannot tell

Answer

64. The media-sanctioned view of young mothers includes the claim that they are incapable of being good parents.

A True
B False
C Cannot tell

Answer

Passage 22

People with hypertension have a 60% greater risk of a heart attack when the temperature is more than five degrees cooler than the previous day's temperature. As well as increasing blood pressure, cold weather can cause blood to thicken and make a clot more likely. Cholesterol levels also increase during cold weather and infections of the respiratory tract are far more common and contribute further to the risk of a heart attack. Hypertension is believed to affect 40% of adults in Northern Europe and very often goes unnoticed until serious damage to a sufferer's health has occurred.

65. Hypertension can cause the blood to thicken and clot during a spell of cold weather.

A True
B False
C Cannot tell

Answer

66. The passage describes the very unlikely situation whereby 40% of adults have a 60% risk of a heart attack when the temperature drops from one day to the next by more than five degrees.

A True
B False
C Cannot tell

Answer

67. More hypertension sufferers have heart attacks during the winter months.

A True
B False
C Cannot tell

Answer

End of test

Test 3: Analysis of information

Test instructions

This test comprises 22 passages and 66 questions.

You are allowed 44 minutes to complete it (almost 40 seconds a question).

You are given a series of passages, each of which is followed by a number of statements. It is your task to say whether the statement is true or false or whether it is not possible to say if the statement is true or false. You should base your decision only on the information or opinions given in the passage.

You should judge the statement to be true only if, for example, it follows logically from the passage or is a rewording of something contained in the passage or is a valid summary of the passage or a part of it.

You should judge the statement to be false if, for example, it cannot follow logically from the passage or if it contradicts something contained in the passage.

If you require more information than is contained in the passage before you can tell if the statement is true or false then you should record your answer as 'cannot tell'.

You should work quickly and not spend too long on any one question.

Work without interruption.

Do not turn over the page until you are ready to begin.

Passage 1

EU national airlines will not make any money on their short-haul European operations this year despite heavy promotions of reduced fares and a campaign to cut costs. Most of these so-called flag carriers have reluctantly decided to pass on soaring fuel costs to short-haul passengers in the form of a surcharge on tickets. At the same time, they are encountering strong competition on most European routes from the budget carriers, who have pledged not to levy surcharges. Budget airlines have dramatically raised their short-haul market share, taking advantage of the financial difficulties at flag carriers. Short-haul accounts for almost one-fourth of the national carriers' business while the remainder is derived from long-haul flights, demand for which has experienced a strong recovery.

1. National airlines have imposed fuel surcharges on long-haul passengers too.

   A True
   B False
   C Cannot tell

   Answer

2. The cost of flying on European routes has fallen.

   A True
   B False
   C Cannot tell

   Answer

3. Losses on short-haul flights are adding to the financial difficulties experienced by national airlines.

   A True
   B False
   C Cannot tell

   Answer

Passage 2

Crude oil stocks are closely monitored by traders to establish the markets' natural supply and demand levels. Hoarding was a major factor in the high crude prices in the 1970s and evidence is again suggesting that hoarding is fuelling current record high crude prices. Crude stocks had fallen because refiners had adopted just-in-time stock management policies. However, traders have noticed that some countries are purchasing oil at levels well above their rate of consumption, suggesting that the hoarding of oil stocks is once again occurring. Traders have recently increased the world's crude markets' assumed levels of demand quite substantially because of increased consumption by developing nations such as India and China.

4. No facts are offered in support of the thesis that current high crude prices are being supported by the hoarding of stock.

   A True
   B False
   C Cannot tell

   Answer

5. If hoarding is supporting high crude prices then one would expect prices to fall back once hoards have been established.

   A True
   B False
   C Cannot tell

   Answer

6. India and China have recently become major oil importers.

   A True
   B False
   C Cannot tell

   Answer

Passage 3

You cannot be very intelligent if you do not know how smart you are until you have been told your IQ rate. It is probably unwise to take an IQ test because if you do then you risk feeling either superior or disappointed when you get the result, and neither of these sentiments is beneficial. What difference would it make to your life anyway, if you were to find out that you have the IQ of a genius or well below average? These considerations did not stop almost half a million Europeans from taking part in an internet IQ test. In the test, men scored 110 while women scored 105; left-handed people scored much higher than right-handed people; and people with brown eyes scored best while people with red hair scored the least.

7. The results suggest that men are more intelligent than women.

A True
B False
C Cannot tell

Answer

8. It is reasonable to surmise that the author would have difficulty understanding why someone would want to know their IQ.

A True
B False
C Cannot tell

Answer

9. The passage is written in a satirical style.

A True
B False
C Cannot tell

Answer

Passage 4

Hybrid cars use half as much fuel as their petrol-only equivalents; a petrol engine is used to drive the wheels and to charge a large battery that powers an electric motor and in turn also drives the wheels. Hybrids cost around $3,500 more than an equivalent petrol car. This high price makes the economics questionable for owners who average 12,000 miles a year as it would mean a 12-year payback; nevertheless, hybrid sales are strong in the United States.

In Europe, hybrid car sales have increased much more slowly. This is due in part to fuel taxes being much higher. The other factor is that European drivers have the option of buying diesel-engine-powered cars, which are almost as fuel efficient as hybrid cars. This possibility is denied to Americans because strict limits on particle emissions mean that diesel engines are effectively banned.

10. The diesel engine is as environmentally advantageous as the hybrid.

A True
B False
C Cannot tell

☐ Answer

11. An economic case for buying a hybrid car might be made in the United States but not in Europe.

A True
B False
C Cannot tell

☐ Answer

12. If the price of fuel at the filling stations were to fall, any economic case for hybrids would improve.

A True
B False
C Cannot tell

Answer

Passage 5

Plastic bags litter our streets, kill wildlife, block drains and remain in the environment for decades. Plastic bags account for less than 1% of the household waste sent to landfill sites. Eighty per cent are recycled at least once as bin liners or are put to some other reuse. They are more energy efficient than alternatives such as paper or cardboard. If they are incinerated in energy from waste plants then some of the energy used in their manufacture can be recovered.

13. Plastic bags have a high reuse rate for a disposable item.

A True
B False
C Cannot tell

Answer

14. Plastic bags are a hygienic and convenient way of carrying things.

A True
B False
C Cannot tell

Answer

15. On balance the passage can be judged as coming down in favour of a case for the banning or taxing of plastic bags.

A True
B False
C Cannot tell

Answer

Passage 6

For 20 consecutive years the pass rate in the national advanced-level exams has increased. The exam questions have not become easier but the students find it easier to obtain top grades now that marks are awarded for course and project work and only 20% of the marks are reserved for the final exams. Last year 130,000 girls obtained two A grades whereas 20 years ago only 34,000 obtained these marks. Before 1987, grades were norm-rated against previous years, with only the top 10% of candidates being awarded an A grade. Since that date no limit to the number of A grades has been set and anyone who scores over 60% receives an A grade. This change has seen the number of A grades awarded more than double.

16. The examining method has made it easier for students to obtain top grades.

A True
B False
C Cannot tell

Answer

17. Girls have been mainly responsible for the rise in the number of A grades.

A True
B False
C Cannot tell

Answer

18. Twenty per cent of candidates now realize a score over 60%.

A True
B False
C Cannot tell

Answer

Passage 7

Many barristers hold that the compensation culture is in fact hype and imagined. They rely on the fact that the number of compensation cases going through the courts is falling. Others believe that they are wrong because the figure excludes the large increase in the numbers of claims brought to industrial tribunals and because they ignore the widespread fear of compensation. A fear of being sued, it is argued, has changed day-to-day life and this is what is meant by the compensation culture. These changes include the cancellation of school outings and the banning of ball games in the park. Bizarre judgments have also added to a sense of compensation culture; an example of such a judgment is the successful case of the prisoner who sued the prison service after he fell from a roof when trying to escape.

19. The case made for the compensation culture is entirely anecdotal.

A True
B False
C Cannot tell

Answer

20. The warnings printed on paper cups stating that the drink inside is hot so we should exercise extreme caution could be used as another example of how the fear of being sued has impacted on everyday life.

A True
B False
C Cannot tell

Answer

21. If you discount claims that originate from employment then the view that we now face a higher risk of a claim for compensation is indeed imagined.

A True
B False
C Cannot tell

Answer

Passage 8

The amount of liquid assets held by non-financial corporations has almost doubled over the past five years. The increase in assets relative to debt is in sharp contrast to the late 1990s, when companies raised large amounts of debt to fund capital investments and acquisitions. The reluctance of companies today to spend, despite the fact that they hold large amounts of cash, shows that they are unwilling to make the mistake again of over-investment leading to production greater than demand. Telecommunications and high-technology companies were among the big spenders then and they suffered its effects more than most; they are now the most thrifty. Drug companies also want to keep cash at hand in order to fund expensive lawsuits should they arise. Other sectors with large workforces are having to hoard cash because they face large pension shortfalls.

22. In the late 1990s, capital spending in the telecommunications and high-technology sectors led to production outstripping supply.

A True
B False
C Cannot tell

Answer

23. Cash at hand is a symptom of a cautious business outlook.

A True
B False
C Cannot tell

Answer

24. The passage implies that over-investment leads to production outstripping demand.

A True
B False
C Cannot tell

Answer

Passage 9

The first salmon farms were in the Atlantic islands but the industry fell into dramatic decline with the value of the farmed fish when the farming method became discredited because of the use of chemicals and concerns over the feed used. Now they are farming cod in the Atlantic isles, only this time they have set rules for fish welfare and are feeding the cod on fish meal produced only from the by-products of fish already caught for human consumption. The enclosure nets in which the fish are grown are cleaned mechanically rather than treated with chemicals to stop them becoming fouled with weed. Cod, unlike salmon, are a gregarious species that naturally shoal and, unlike salmon, they do not need to be treated with insecticide to control fish lice.

25. A gregarious species of fish will be happier to swim around a net enclosure with a lot of other fish.

A True
B False
C Cannot tell

Answer

26. The cod farmers are taking measures to avoid the mistakes of the salmon farmers.

A True
B False
C Cannot tell

Answer

27. Measures are being taken to raise the cod humanely.

A True
B False
C Cannot tell

Answer

Passage 10

Nuclear power is carbon free and new nuclear power plants do produce less radioactive waste than the older ones but the problem still exists, so building new nuclear power stations would address the long-term environmental problem of carbon emissions but only by exacerbating another problem. Critics complain of the visual intrusion caused by the renewable power stations, but appropriate planning can limit this and it is reversible. Nuclear power's electricity is expensive when compared with carbon-producing gas or coal plants. Renewable energy sources when compared with nuclear are relatively cheap and have the potential to become cheaper.

28. A very good environmental case for nuclear power could be made if the problem of radioactive waste could be solved.

A True
B False
C Cannot tell

Answer

29. Alternatives to nuclear that are carbon-free power sources have problems of their own.

A True
B False
C Cannot tell

Answer

30. Renewable power is carbon free.

A True
B False
C Cannot tell

Answer

Passage 11

Accountants are pressing the government to allow them a client confidentiality defence if they suspect a client of money laundering or tax avoidance. The government is relying on new legislation concerning the issue of disclosure by lawyers and accountants to make substantial cuts in both money hidden by criminals and the amount of unpaid tax. Consultation has begun about giving accountants the same protection as lawyers on the issue of laundering but the government has rejected claims that lawyers have any more protection than accountants on the issue of disclosing tax avoidance.

31. There are two issues at stake and it would seem that the current rules are different for lawyers and accountants.

A True
B False
C Cannot tell

Answer

32. The legislation will require lawyers and accountants to provide confidential information to the government about all their clients.

A True
B False
C Cannot tell

Answer

33. The accountants want parity with lawyers.

A True
B False
C Cannot tell

Answer

Passage 12

The most commonly cited reasons for companies to use the internet for recruitment were cost-effectiveness, ease of use and the potential to access a larger number of candidates. In the past year the number of organizations using the internet to fill jobs has risen by almost a third. Now 12 million job seekers are expected to apply online in the UK each year. In the United States 51% of all jobs were advertised online; the UK figure is around 27%, so analysts feel that there is still considerable growth left in the UK market. The age of online recruitment seems to have arrived, but many companies are using it only as one part of a multimedia recruitment strategy.

34. To be sure to access an even larger number of candidates a company must advertise vacancies on the internet as well as through more traditional media.

A True
B False
C Cannot tell

Answer

35. The majority of UK jobs are now advertised on the internet.

A True
B False
C Cannot tell

Answer

36. One reason for online recruitment's popularity is because it represents good value.

A True
B False
C Cannot tell

Answer

Passage 13

Under 5% of employers test their staff for the use of recreational drugs and the vast majority do not consider substance abuse to be a significant issue in their workplace. Evidence of a link between drug abuse and accidents or low productivity is hard to find. More studies found a link between alcoholism and a detrimental impact on safety and performance than a link with drugs, either so-called soft drugs such as cannabis or class 1 drugs such as cocaine. Employers face problems if they decide that they should test staff for drugs. In addition to ethical considerations, employees have a right to privacy under the Human Rights Act; however, the employer also has a duty to provide a safe workplace and has a duty of care to take every reasonable step to ensure safety at work under the Health and Safety at Work Act. In some industries, for example the transport and nuclear power industries, employers do routinely test their staff for drug use.

37. There is evidence that the use of recreational drugs is irrelevant to most employers.

A True
B False
C Cannot tell

Answer

38. There is no conflict between the right to privacy and the right to a safe place of work.

A True
B False
C Cannot tell

Answer

39. Society cannot afford the risk of an accident caused by an employee on drugs in the transport or nuclear industry and that is why testing takes place in those industries.

A True
B False
C Cannot tell

Answer

Passage 14

We are such optimists and opportunists that we find it hard not to adopt every new technology as soon as it comes along. As a result, we tend to discover the adverse consequences of these new practices the hard way. When problems emerge, as they inevitably seem to do, we set about a search for a better technology to help solve or alleviate the problems created by the first. However, some commentators argue that the debate over the introduction of new technology to generically modify crops was not about an existing technology but about a proposed one, and for once they claim we tried to identify the benefits and risks before running blindly into them. The example is held up as a new way of assessing technologies before adopting them, and governments are urged to require companies to test and environmentally model new technologies before they are introduced. The difficulty with such a recommendation to governments is that not all will adopt them and most new technologies are introduced by multinational companies that exist beyond the control of one or a few governments. These companies therefore can choose to avoid new controls over their commercial activities by simply taking their developmental work elsewhere.

40. Environmental problems such as acid rain or ozone depletion might have been avoided had the new approach been adopted in the past.

A True
B False
C Cannot tell

Answer

41. If our government were to adopt the recommendation then we could look forward to no longer lurching from one failed technology to the next.

A True
B False
C Cannot tell

Answer

42. Some governments are already requiring companies to test and environmentally model the impact of new technologies before introducing them.

A True
B False
C Cannot tell

Answer

Passage 15

Researchers believe that there is growing evidence to support the hypothesis that attention deficit hyperactivity disorder (ADHD) should not be dismissed as ordinary bad behaviour but should be recognized as a serious childhood disease. It is claimed that as many as one in five children are at risk of suffering this condition, which is linked to an increased risk of serious illness in adulthood. The disease is not caused by bad parenting, but a chaotic or difficult home environment in a child's early years activates the syndrome where there already exists a genetic predisposition. If left untreated, sufferers were found to be four times more likely to suffer from mental illness as young adults.

43. ADHD is triggered by specific environmental circumstances.

A True
B False
C Cannot tell

Answer

44. It can be inferred from the passage that as many as one in five young children suffer a chaotic or difficult home environment.

A True
B False
C Cannot tell

Answer

45. Children with ADHD are more likely to suffer mental illness as young adults.

 A True
 B False
 C Cannot tell

Answer

Passage 16

If the number of extra households in London rises at the rate suggested then house prices in that capital city are predicted to rise even further and pull further ahead still of house prices in the rest of the UK. Relative to the UK average, house prices in the capital have dropped back to their lowest level for more than five years. The rapid growth in the number of people wanting to live in London over the next two decades suggests that this trend is likely to be reversed. In the short term the trend of prices rising further in the rest of the country relative to London is expected to continue.

46. In real terms houses are cheaper in London than they were five years ago.

 A True
 B False
 C Cannot tell

Answer

47. In 20 years' time the price of a house in London is expected to rise faster than the price of houses in the rest of the UK.

 A True
 B False
 C Cannot tell

Answer

48. A widening divide between the price of houses in the capital and the rest of the country will be driven by high levels of demand for housing.

A True
B False
C Cannot tell

Answer

Passage 17

In the 1950s, nitrates – preservative used in processed meats and occurring naturally in green foods – were linked to stomach cancer. More recently, biologists are claiming a positive role for dietary nitrates. Concerns were first raised when high doses of a nitrate compound commonly present in the stomach were found to cause cancer in laboratory rats. But the findings of this early study could not be consistently repeated, and the results of a great many subsequent epidemiological studies found no link between nitrates and human stomach cancer. The discovery of a positive role began with the realization that our stomachs hold large amounts of nitrate oxide and it was proposed that this agent may be helping to kill bacteria in our food such as *E. coli*. Stomach acid has for decades been considered the body's main means of killing dangerous germs in our diet. But it was found that stomach acid and nitrate oxide when mixed together killed such germs much more quickly.

49. A compound of nitrate is carcinogenic.

A True
B False
C Cannot tell

Answer

50. A relationship between the ingestion of nitrates and human stomach cancer has not been substantiated.

A True
B False
C Cannot tell

Answer

51. Dietary nitrate, far from being a risk to health, is in fact an important natural defence against infections.

A True
B False
C Cannot tell

Answer

Passage 18

Faced with the spiralling costs of medical care and double-digit increases in premiums for the fifth year running, American insurers and employers who offer employee medical cover are desperately looking for innovative ways to tackle the astronomical cost of medical insurance in the United States. One initiative that is proving effective involves encouraging employees to undertake health risk assessments and then following the assessment up with help to adjust lifestyles in order to reduce any identified risks. The idea is that such preventive measures will stop conditions from developing in the first place and reduce the need for future expensive interventions. Employees are encouraged to take much more responsibility for their own medical care and the cost of it. This is achieved by offering sufferers with known conditions incentives if they attend specialist centres set up by the insurers to manage the condition rather than doing nothing until the condition becomes chronic and they then require much more expensive general hospital care.

52. The new approach is described as involving a degree of compulsion.

A True
B False
C Cannot tell

Answer

53. All consumers of health care benefit from this initiative.

A True
B False
C Cannot tell

Answer

54. Under the initiative an employee who smokes might be offered help to give up so that, if the insured person is successful in stopping, the insurance company will avoid the further cost of providing treatment for the many harmful effects of smoking.

A True
B False
C Cannot tell

Answer

Passage 19

The car of 2020 will probably have a hydrogen-powered cell to charge batteries that drive the wheels. The thermodynamic efficiency of this vehicle will be around 60% compared with an efficiency of 23% for the typical car being driven around on our roads today and it will have a range of 500 kilometres between fuel stops. Currently the best published fuel cell thermodynamic efficiency is claimed by an experimental vehicle in the United States with an efficiency of 39%; this compares with 40% for the most efficient internal combustion diesel-powered production car currently on the market. In the foretold hydrogen economy, accidents in which hydrogen is released into the environment will be far more commonplace, and hydrogen is a very potent greenhouse gas. Proponents of a hydrogen economy argue that leaks and emissions would in fact not pose catastrophic damage to the environment because the hydrogen infrastructure of production and storage would be far more centralized than the current petroleum infrastructure and this would mean that the monitoring and repair of leaks and emissions could be better managed and technological upgrades could be more readily implemented.

55. The overall benefits of hydrogen currently seem lacking.

    A True
    B False
    C Cannot tell

    Answer

56. A hydrogen economy would be worse for the environment than the current petroleum economy.

    A True
    B False
    C Cannot tell

    Answer

57. The passage is supportive of the development of an automotive fuel cell.

A True
B False
C Cannot tell

Answer

Passage 20

A deterioration of adolescents' mental health over the past 25 years has been reported. The rate of emotional problems such as anxiety and depression has increased by 60% among teenagers. Girls in particular are more likely to suffer emotional problems but the rate at which these problems have increased is far higher among boys. The increase is not explained by the increase in single parenthood. The increases were found across all types of family. Nor can the deterioration be put down to greater inequality, as again the rate of problems reported was consistent across social class. No differences were found in racial origin using a representative sample of adolescents suffering these problems from all the major ethnic groups.

58. The research is an example of a time trend study.

A True
B False
C Cannot tell

Answer

59. The findings highlight a very widespread malaise.

A True
B False
C Cannot tell

Answer

60. The possible causes of the sharp decline in teenage health are not considered.

A True
B False
C Cannot tell

Answer

Passage 21

A link between demographics and savings is sometimes based on a theory of investment that runs thus: young people borrow, middle-aged people save and the elderly draw from their savings. According to this theory, borrowing should be highest when a population is disproportionately young, and savings should be highest when that disproportional cohort reaches middle age.

61. When a population is disproportionately young, the cost of borrowing will be high and the yield from a low rate of saving will be high.

A True
B False
C Cannot tell

Answer

62. According to the theory, a high level of savings must mean that a population is disproportionately middle-aged.

A True
B False
C Cannot tell

Answer

63. When a population is disproportionately middle-aged then the cost of borrowing will fall and the supply of savings will rise and the yield of those savings will fall.

A True
B False
C Cannot tell

Answer

Passage 22

The newly deployed ground-based mid-course missile defence system comprises 10 interceptor missiles, each of which is intended to collide in outer space with an incoming hostile missile. So far in field trials the system has successfully intercepted target missiles in five out of eight flight tests. Critics say that these trials prove very little. Live tests are very expensive, take a great deal of organization and are usually limited by concerns over safety (you really do not want one of these missiles going astray and crashing into a city centre, for example). For these reasons, a lot of the development programme has relied on models and simulations rather than real flight tests. Both critics and supporters of the programme accept that these models do a far better job of predicting the performance of system components than of predicting the performance of the system overall.

64. So far only eight tests have been conducted.

A True
B False
C Cannot tell

Answer

65. The primary verification tool for the efficiency of the missile defence system has been virtual.

A True
B False
C Cannot tell

Answer

66. Simulation and theoretical models cannot capture all the variables that can occur in a real missile engagement.

A True
B False
C Cannot tell

Answer

End of test

4

Tests 4, 5 and 6: Data interpretation

This chapter comprises 242 questions organized as three realistic practice tests. These tests provide a realistic experience of the challenge real graduate numeracy tests represent in terms of both the question types and the sheer hard work and sustained concentration demanded.

So many graduate numerical tests require you both to be competent in the key mathematical operations and to demonstrate that you can reason with figures with or without a calculator. Even when you are allowed a calculator, a well-practised candidate will often be quicker without one and, importantly, will know if under the pressure of the test they have mis-keyed a sum. So put the calculator away and undertake this practice without one!

This chapter is intended for the vast majority of graduates who have not needed to apply their numeracy skills in an exam-type situation since their GCSEs. It seeks to build confidence in the key competencies and assist in the development of the skills, speed and accuracy necessary to survive a real graduate psychometric test of numerical skills.

A major focus of the material is on the operation of percentages. Above all other mathematical operations, in tests used to select graduates and managers across a wide range of industries you are expected to demonstrate complete competence in this operation, such as calculating percentage increase or decrease and percentage profit or loss. Another operation covered in some detail is ratios.

The material in this chapter will lead you up to the level of competence required by graduate tests in these key operations. More advanced material can be found in the Kogan Page titles *How to Pass Advanced Numeracy Tests* and *The Advanced Numeracy Test Workbook*. More elementary material can be found in the titles *How to Pass Numeracy Tests* and *How to Pass Numerical Reasoning Tests*.

If you are numerically accomplished then you may still find this chapter of practical use by attempting the tests in the lower of the recommended times allowed. This level of question will represent the bulk of the material found in the numerical sub-tests that you face. Practice in it represents, therefore, the opportunity for you to force home your advantage by obtaining maximum marks in the minimum time, leaving you able to concentrate on any more challenging material examined in a real test.

Test 4: Data interpretation

Test instructions

This test comprises 100 questions.

You should attempt all the questions in:

Maximum recommended time 1 hour 15 minutes (45 seconds a question)
Minimum recommended time 50 minutes (if you intend to do this test this quickly then you should have already realized how long this allows you to attempt each question!)

To do well in this test you must avoid spending too long on any one question and work quickly and hard. You will also have to sustain a high level of concentration over an extended time.

Each question requires you to write a short answer in a box provided.

Answers and many explanations are provided on pages 187–195.

An interpretation of your score is provided on pages 211–213.

You should be able to do these questions without a calculator.

Work without interruption

Do not turn over the page until you are ready to begin.

1. What is 30% of 55? Answer

2. What is 80% of 12? Answer

3. What is 5% of 450? Answer

4. What is 17% of 15? Answer

5. What is 22% of 175? Answer

6. What is 38% of 60? Answer

7. What is 11% of 220? Answer

8. What is 90% of 480? Answer

9. What is 57% of 75? Answer

10. What is 74% of 360? Answer

11. What is 60% of 98? ☐ Answer

12. What is 23% of 330? ☐ Answer

13. What is 56% of 0.5? ☐ Answer

14. What is 7% of 580? ☐ Answer

15. What is 36% of 90? ☐ Answer

16. What is 13% of 70? ☐ Answer

17. What is 41% of 160? ☐ Answer

18. What is 14% of 45? ☐ Answer

19. What is 84% of 84? ☐ Answer

20. What is 50p as a percentage of £25? ☐ Answer

21. What is 100 ml as a percentage of 2 litres? Answer

22. What is six minutes as a percentage of two hours? Answer

23. What is 500 cm as a percentage of 1 km? Answer

24. What is 25p as a percentage of £100? Answer

25. What is 26 weeks as a percentage of four years? Answer

26. What is 45 metres as a percentage of 2 kilometres? Answer

27. What is 50 grams as a percentage of 4 kilos? Answer

28. What is 30 minutes expressed as a percentage of 8 hours? Answer

29. What is 40 gm as a percentage of 10 kilograms? Answer

30. What is 75p as a percentage of £50? Answer

31. What is 30 seconds as a percentage of 1 hour 40 minutes?

Answer

32. What is 400 mm as a percentage of 12 metres? (Express your answer to two decimal places.)

Answer

33. What is 168 metres as a percentage of 1.2 kilometres?

Answer

34. What is 7.3 days as a percentage of a non-leap year?

Answer

35. What is £1.80 as a percentage of £45?

Answer

36. Find 45 as a percentage of 200.

Answer

37. Find 630 as a percentage of 700.

Answer

38. Find 31.5 as a percentage of 126.

Answer

39. Find 5.4 as a percentage of 90.

Answer

40. Find 32 as a percentage of 96.
(Express your answer to 4 sf.)

Answer

41. Find 144 as a percentage of 450.

Answer

42. Find 135 as a percentage of 300.

Answer

43. Find 72 as a percentage of 360.

Answer

44. Find 42.5 as a percentage of 250.

Answer

45. Find 665 as a percentage of 1,900.

Answer

46. Find 10 as a percentage of 60.
(Express your answer to 3 sf.)

Answer

47. Find 21 as a percentage of 140.

Answer

48. Find 17 as a percentage of 20.

Answer

49. Find 24 as a percentage of 64.

Answer

50. Find 11 as a percentage of 40. ☐ Answer

51. Find 360 as a percentage of 450. ☐ Answer

52. Find 165 as a percentage of 400. ☐ Answer

53. Find 120 as a percentage of 250. ☐ Answer

54. Find 1,200 as a percentage of 1,600. ☐ Answer

55. Find 19.2 as a percentage of 80. ☐ Answer

56. An item is decreased from £8 to £6.
What is the percentage change? ☐ Answer

57. An item is increased from £60 to £78.
Find the percentage change. ☐ Answer

58. An item is decreased to £28 from £70.
What is the percentage change? ☐ Answer

59. An item is increased to £87 from £75.
Find the percentage change. ☐ Answer

60. What is the percentage decrease between 15 and 12? ☐ Answer

61. Find the percentage increase between 24 and 27. ☐ Answer

62. An item is decreased from £83 to £24.90.
What is the percentage change? ☐ Answer

63. An item is increased from £8 to £11.20.
Find the percentage change. ☐ Answer

64. An item is decreased to £26.40 from £44.
What is the percentage change? ☐ Answer

65. An item is increased to £52.90 from £46.
Find the percentage change. ☐ Answer

66. What is the percentage change between 69 and 55.2? ☐ Answer

67. A price is increased from 36p to 45p.
Find the percentage change.

Answer

68. A price is decreased from £23 to £18.40.
What is the percentage change?

Answer

69. A price is increased to £15.60 from £12.
Find the percentage change.

Answer

70. A price is decreased to £75.60 from £90.
What is the percentage change?

Answer

71. A price is increased from £74 to £77.70.
Find the percentage change.

Answer

72. A price is decreased from £52.25 to £55.
What is the percentage change?

Answer

73. A figure is increased from 7 to 13.3.
Find the percentage change.

Answer

74. A figure is increased from 14 to 23.8.
Find the percentage change.

Answer

75. A figure is decreased from 36 to 31.5. What is the percentage change?

Answer

76. An item was bought for 15p and sold for 12p. What was the percentage profit or loss?

Answer

77. An item was bought for 30p and sold for 42p. What was the percentage profit or loss?

Answer

78. An item was bought for £40 and sold for £42. What was the percentage profit or loss?

Answer

79. An item was bought for £800 and sold for £72. What was the percentage profit or loss?

Answer

80. An item was bought for £70 and sold for £72.10. What was the percentage profit or loss?

Answer

81. An item was bought for £55 and sold for £31.90. What was the percentage profit or loss?

Answer

82. An item was bought for £17.80 and sold for £20.47. What was the percentage profit or loss?

Answer

83. An item was bought for £40.40 and sold for £10.10. What was the percentage profit or loss?

Answer

84. An item was bought for £75 and sold for £93.75. What was the percentage profit or loss?

Answer

85. An item was bought for £110 and sold for £100.10. What was the percentage profit or loss?

Answer

86. Divide 150 into the ratio 2 : 3.

Answer

87. Divide 90 into the ratio 1 : 4.

Answer

88. Divide 96 into the ratio 7 : 1.

Answer

89. Divide 135 into the ratio 2 : 7.

Answer

90. Divide 180 into the ratio 5 : 4.

Answer

91. Divide 117 into the ratio 6 : 3.

Answer

92. Divide 200 into the ratio 3 : 5. ☐ Answer

93. Divide 450 into the ratio 3: 2 : 4. ☐ Answer

94. Divide 270 into the ratio 2 : 3 : 1. ☐ Answer

95. Divide 192 into the ratio 9 : 7 : 8. ☐ Answer

96. Divide 1,320 into the ratio 8 : 3 : 11. ☐ Answer

97. Divide 85 into the ratio 2 : 6 : 9. ☐ Answer

98. Divide 168 into the ratio 7 : 2 : 5. ☐ Answer

99. Divide 128 into the ratio 3 : 9 : 4. ☐ Answer

100. Divide 1,800 into the ratio 4 : 5 : 1. ☐ Answer

End of test

Test 5: Data interpretation

Test instructions

This test comprises 75 questions. They build on the competencies developed in the previous test and continue to assist in the development of the skills, speed and accuracy necessary to do well in a real graduate psychometric numerical test.

Maximum recommended time 1 hour 15 minutes (one minute a question)
Minimum recommended time 50 minutes (40 seconds a question)

To do well in this test you must avoid spending too long on any one question and work quickly and hard.

Each question requires you to select one of the suggested answers and to write it in a box provided.

Answers and many explanations are provided on pages 195–201.

An interpretation of your score is provided on pages 213–215.

You should be able to do these questions without a calculator.

Work without interruption.

Do not turn over the page until you are ready to begin.

1. A ratio in its simplest form comprises only whole numbers that have no common factor other than 1. Express 63 : 18 as a ratio in its simplest form.

A 6 : 2
B 7 : 2
C 8 : 2
D 9 : 2

Answer

2. Express 27 : 54 as a ratio in its simplest form.

A 1 : 2
B 2 : 3
C 3 : 4
D 2 : 5

Answer

3. Express 15 : 9 as a ratio in its simplest form.

A 2 : 1
B 3 : 2
C 4 : 3
D 5 : 3

Answer

4. Express 54 : 24 as a ratio in its simplest form.

A 6 : 5
B 7 : 4
C 8 : 3
D 9 : 4
E 9 : 5

Answer

5. Express 28 : 32 as a ratio in its simplest form.

A 5 : 3
B 6 : 5
C 7 : 8
D 8 : 7

☐ Answer

6. Express 13 : 39 as a ratio in its simplest form.

A 1 : 3
B 1 : 5
C 2 : 3
D 3 : 7

☐ Answer

7. Express 14 : 49 as a ratio in its simplest form.

A 7 : 2
B 6 : 11
C 3 : 8
D 2 : 7

☐ Answer

8. Express 15 : 3 as a ratio in its simplest form.

A 4 : 1
B 5 : 1
C 6 : 1
D 7 : 1

☐ Answer

9. Express 72 : 60 as a ratio in its simplest form.

A 5 : 7
B 6 : 7
C 6 : 5
D 7 : 6

Answer

10. Express 20 : 25 as a ratio in its simplest form.

A 1 : 5
B 2 : 5
C 3 : 5
D 4 : 5

Answer

11. Express 9 : 6 : 12 as a ratio in its simplest form.

A 3 : 3 : 6
B 3 : 2 : 4
C 3 : 1 : 4
D 3 : 2 : 3

Answer

12. Express 20 : 30 : 5 as a ratio in its simplest form.

A 4 : 6 : 1
B 5 : 3 : 1
C 2 : 3 : 0.5
D 4 : 5 : 1

Answer

13. Express 32 : 8 : 12 as a ratio in its simplest form.

A 5 : 4 : 6
B 16 : 4 : 6
C 8 : 2 : 3
D 7 : 3 : 4

Answer

14. Express 45 : 18 : 9 as a ratio in its simplest form.

A 15 : 6 : 3
B 5 : 2 : 1
C 9 : 6 : 3
D 7 : 6 : 3

Answer

15. Express 54 : 6 : 30 as a ratio in its simplest form.

A 9 : 1 : 5
B 6 : 3 : 15
C 8 : 2 : 3
D 7 : 3 : 10

Answer

16. A salesperson receives 8% commission on the value of sales. How much commission is due on £4,550?

A £364
B £365
C £366
D £367

Answer

17. If the value of a computer depreciates by 6% each year, how much is a £650 computer worth after two years?

A £574.32
B £574.33
C £574.34
D £574.35

Answer

18. A carpet when laid stretches 5%. If after being laid it measures 63 m long, how long was it before being fitted?

A 58 m
B 9 m
C 60 m
D 61 m

Answer

19. After selling 40% of his original holding, a property developer is left with 3 acres of land. How much did he originally own?

A 3 acres
B 4 acres
C 5 acres
D 6 acres

Answer

20. A suite of furniture is advertised at £690 after a 15% price increase. What was the original price?

A £590
B £600
C £610
D £620

Answer

21. If the working week were to be decreased from 35 to 28 hours, what percentage decrease would this represent?

A 17%
B 18%
C 19%
D 20%

Answer

22. Two items are bought for £5.00 and sold individually for £3.10 each. What is the percentage profit?

A 23%
B 24%
C 25%
D 26%

Answer

23. The time taken to complete an order increases by 15 minutes to 5 hours 15 minutes. What is the percentage increase?

A 5%
B 6%
C 7%
D 8%

Answer

24. A commercial rent of £3,200 is decreased to £3,008. What percentage decrease in income does the landlord suffer?

A 4%
B 5%
C 6%
D 7%

Answer

25. An investment is found to increase by 12% to £1,008. What was the original amount invested?

A £900
B £910
C £920
D £930

Answer

26. In a survey, 3,200 people took part, of whom 1,280 were aged 65 or over. What percentage of respondents belonged to this cohort?

A 30%
B 35%
C 40%
D 45%

Answer

27. A company with 32 employees makes 12 redundant. What percentage reduction in employees is this?

A 36.5%
B 37%
C 37.5%
D 38%

Answer

28. An investment increases in value from £220 to £253. What percentage increase is this?

A 14%
B 15%
C 16%
D 17%

Answer

29. If a jar of coffee normally contains 320 grams and a special-offer jar contains 15% more, how many extra grams of coffee does the special-offer jar contain?

A 48 grams
B 49 grams
C 50 grams
D 51 grams

☐ Answer

30. If a company increases its turnover from £180,000 to £234,000, what is the percentage increase?

A 28%
B 29%
C 30%
D 31%

☐ Answer

31. If a salary is increased from £25,000 to £26,750, what is the percentage increase?

A 6%
B 7%
C 8%
D 9%

☐ Answer

32. The number of contracts awarded by a government department is found to have fallen from 3,200 to 2,336. What is this decrease expressed as a percentage?

A 27%
B 26%
C 25%
D 24%

☐ Answer

33. A cinema has a capacity of 480 seats. If it is 80% full, how many seats are unoccupied?

A 93
B 94
C 95
D 96

Answer

34. A town's population of 14,000 is found to be increasing by 5% a year. What will the new population be after two years?

A 15,435
B 15,354
C 15,543
D 15,534

Answer

35. An hourly wage is increased by 5% to £5.88. How much was the rate before the increase?

A £5.60
B £5.70
C £5.80
D £5.90

Answer

36. In a sale an item is reduced by 20% on the normal price of £76.50. What is the sale price?

A £61.50
B £61.40
C £61.30
D £61.20

Answer

37. A tin of flour weighs 350 grams, 40% of which is flour. How many grams of flour does the tin contain?

A 135 grams
B 140 grams
C 145 grams
D 150 grams

Answer

38. If a job costs £400 to deliver but is only charged at £324, what is the percentage loss?

A 17%
B 18%
C 19%
D 20%

Answer

39. £2,400 commission is paid at 6% of the value of sales. What was the value of sales to generate the commission figure?

A £39,900
B £40,000
C £40,100
D £40,200

Answer

40. If a commodity goes up from $23 to $36.80, how much is the increase expressed as a percentage?

A 60%
B 61%
C 62%
D 63%

Answer

41. It takes 3 litres of paint to cover an area of 24 square metres. What percentage increase in the quantity of paint would be required to cover an area of 50.4 square metres?

A 90%
B 100%
C 110%
D 120%

Answer

42. A trade discount of 7.5% is given on all purchases. If the value of the discount is worth £19.50, how much was the original value of the goods?

A £245
B £250
C £255
D £260

Answer

43. From a total sample of 7,500, 4,875 responses were received. What percentage response rate is this?

A 65%
B 60%
C 55%
D 50%

Answer

44. Of the people staying at a hotel, 80% arrived by car. If there were 480 guests, how many travelled this way?

A 383
B 384
C 385
D 386

Answer

45. If a total shopping bill is £210, of which £31.50 was spent on food items, what percentage of the total was spent on non-food items?

A 85%
B 80%
C 75%
D 70%

Answer

46. If a 6% increase in salary is received and the new salary level is £371, what was the salary before the increase?

A £320
B £330
C £340
D £350

Answer

47. If a garage sells 42,000 litres of fuel each week and 14,000 litres of this is diesel, what whole-number percentage of all sales are diesel?

A 30%
B 31%
C 32%
D 33%

Answer

48. A cereal was found to contain 15% fibre. How many grams of fibre would be found in a 125-gram serving?

A 18.50 grams
B 18.75 grams
C 19.00 grams
D 19.25 grams

Answer

49. If a new car that cost £8,325 has lost 30% of its value, by how much has its value fallen?

A £2,297.50
B £2,397.50
C £2,497.50
D £2,597.50

Answer

50. A health centre survey found that 45% of patients travelled less than one mile to the surgery. If 8,800 patients took part in the survey, how many of the respondents travelled less than one mile to see their doctor?

A 3,960
B 4,010
C 4,060
D 4,120

Answer

51. A loss adjuster recommended to an insurance company that they only pay 37% of a claim for £50,000. If they take the advice, how much will the company pay out?

A £18,300
B £18,500
C £18,800
D £19,100

Answer

52. A total shopping bill is £250, of which £42.50 is tax. What percentage of the total spend is tax?

A 15%
B 16%
C 17%
D 18%

Answer ☐

53. A survey found that 14% of respondents watched a particular TV programme. If 7,500 people took part in the survey, how many respondents reported that they did not watch the programme?

A 6,450
B 6,500
C 6,550
D 6,600

Answer ☐

54. If an item is reduced in a sale by 18% and it would have cost £36.00, how much do you save on the sale price?

A £6.36
B £6.40
C £6.44
D £6.48

Answer ☐

55. An order for a 37.5-metre length of carpet is reduced by 4.5 metres. What percentage reduction in the original order does this represent?

A 12%
B 11%
C 10%
D 9%

Answer ☐

56. If a 100-gram bar of chocolate contains 21 grams of fat and this is 40% of the recommended daily intake, what is the recommended daily intake of fat?

A 51.0 grams
B 51.5 grams
C 52.0 grams
D 52.5 grams

☐ Answer

57. If each month an employee earns £1,800 net and spends £630 on rent, what percentage of his wage does he spend on this essential?

A 35%
B 36%
C 37%
D 38%

☐ Answer

58. If a restaurant served 450 dinners and of these 360 were the chicken special, what percentage of the diners ate the special?

A 75%
B 80%
C 85%
D 90%

☐ Answer

59. If a wage bill is increased from £18,000 to £20,160, what is the percentage increase?

A 12%
B 11%
C 10%
D 9%

☐ Answer

60. If 15 biscuits weigh 90 grams and the weight of each biscuit is 22% butter, what is the weight of butter in one of the biscuits?

A 1.32 grams
B 1.31 grams
C 1.30 grams
D 1.29 grams

Answer

61. If a company enjoys a profit margin of 27%, what is the annual turnover in a year when £24,300 was reported as profit?

A £88,000
B £89,000
C £90,000
D £91,000

Answer

62. If a salesman receives 8% commission on all sales and his sales have increased from £12,500 to £15,950, how much more commission will he receive?

A £273
B £274
C £275
D £276

Answer

63. In May last year total sales were £630,000, and in June that year they increased to £693,000. In the current year total sales in May were £84,000, and in June they increased to £90,720. Which year experienced the greatest percentage increase between May and June?

A Last year
B This year

Answer

64. On a management course attended by 440 delegates, 66 worked for private companies while 100 were freelance. What percentage worked for private companies?

A 15%
B 14%
C 13%
D 12%

Answer

65. Of a sample of 800, 45% were found to be men and 30% women aged 30 or under. How many women are there in the sample aged over 30?

A 160
B 180
C 200
D 220

Answer

66. The values of two funds are in the ratio of 7 : 9. If the value of the smaller fund is £6,300, what is the value of the larger fund?

A £7,800
B £7,900
C £8,000
D £8,100

Answer

67. A company employs 72 staff; the ratio of full-time to part-time staff is 5 : 3. How many full-time staff are there?

A 24
B 32
C 45
D 48

Answer

68. The ratio of successful loan applicants to unsuccessful applicants is 4 : 5. If there are 80 unsuccessful applicants, how many succeeded?

A 64
B 48
C 32
D 16

Answer

69. A production process uses materials in the ratio of 5 : 2. If 1,500 units of material A are used in a shift, how many units of B will remain if at the start of the shift the store held 800?

A 150
B 200
C 250
D 300

Answer

70. The ratio of service to manufacturing businesses in a town is 2 : 3. What is the percentage of service businesses in the town?

A 20%
B 30%
C 40%
D 50%

Answer

71. Three investors A, B and C contribute £3,000, £4,500 and £10,500 to a business. A dividend of £4,800 is awarded and is shared in the ratio of the original investments. How much of the dividend does investor A receive?

A £800
B £820
C £840
D £860

Answer

72. A journal records a transaction of £336 in the ratio of 5 : 3. What is the value of the lesser sum?

A £123
B £124
C £125
D £126

Answer

73. If a company were to pay £900 tax on £2,700, how much tax would you expect it to pay on £15,000?

A £5,000
B £3,750
C £3,950
D £4,150

Answer

74. Calculate the probability ratio (a comparison between the value of sales and net profit) if a company's sales total £210,000 and its net profit £140,000. (Express the ratio in its simplest form.)

A 7:2
B 6:1
C 5:2
D 3:2

Answer

75. If a company wins 3 out of every 7 proposals made and it needs to win on average 12 proposals a year, how many proposals must be written in a 12-month period?

A 28
B 29
C 30
D 31

Answer

End of test

Test 6: Data interpretation

Test instructions

This test comprises 67 questions. The questions build on the competencies developed in the previous tests and continue to assist in the development of the skills, speed and accuracy necessary to do well in a real graduate psychometric numeracy test. To answer the final 40 questions you must interpret the information provided in text, tables and graphs.

Maximum recommended time 1 hour 8 minutes
Minimum recommended time 50 minutes

To do well in this test you must avoid spending too long on any one question and work quickly and hard.

Each question requires you to write the correct answer into an answer box; some but not all questions provide you with a choice of suggested answers.

Answers and many explanations are provided on pages 202–208.
An interpretation of your score is provided on pages 213–215.
You should not need to use a calculator.
Work without interruption.
Do not turn over the page until you are ready to begin.

1. Calculate the profitability ratio (a comparison between the value of sales and net profit) for a product that achieves a net profit of 18 million on sales of 72 million (express the ratio in its simplest form).

A 3 : 1
B 4 : 1
C 5 : 1
D 6 : 1

☐ Answer

2. Divide 20 by 400.

A 0.5
B 0.05
C 0.005
D 0.0005

☐ Answer

3. A production process uses materials A, B and C in the ratio of 4 : 2 : 1. If an order is received for 1,050 kg of the finished product, how much of material A is required?

A 450 kg
B 500 kg
C 550 kg
D 600 kg

☐ Answer

4. A journal records a transaction of £605, which is posted between two headings in the ratio of 7 : 4. What is the amount of the larger value?

A 385
B 386
C 387
D 388

☐ Answer

5. Divide 7 by 50.

A 0.14
B 0.15
C 0.16
D 0.17

Answer

6. Calculate the profitability ratio (in its simplest form) if net profit of 2.1 million is realized on sales totalling 35 million.

A 30 : 7
B 40 : 5
C 50 : 3
D 60 : 1

Answer

7. Divide 9 by 12.

A 0.60
B 0.65
C 0.70
D 0.75

Answer

8. If monthly sales comprise in thousands 525 for white goods and 840 for brown goods, what is the ratio of the value of brown to white goods sold (expressed in its simplest form)?

A 6 : 1
B 7 : 3
C 8 : 5
D 9 : 4

Answer

9. Divide 12 by 300.

   A 0.03
   B 0.04
   C 0.05
   D 0.06

   ☐ Answer

10. Against a portfolio of 5,000 household insurance policies, 20 claims for flood damage have been received. Express in its simplest form the rate at which this type of claim has occurred.

    A 1 in 200
    B 1 in 250
    C 1 in 300
    D 1 in 350

    ☐ Answer

11. Divide 60 by 250.

    A 0.24
    B 0.25
    C 0.26
    D 0.27

    ☐ Answer

12. A training budget of £6,000 is to be split between two departments so that one department gets three times as much as the other. How much does the better-off department get?

    A £3,000
    B £3,500
    C £4,000
    D £4,500

    ☐ Answer

13. Divide 8 by 25.

A 0.31
B 0.32
C 0.33
D 0.34

Answer

14. Depreciation of £3,700 must be apportioned between A and B in the ratio of 3 : 7. How much will be posted against the budget of department B?

A £2,600
B £2,590
C £2,580
D £2,570

Answer

15. Divide 5 by 40.

A 0.123
B 0.125
C 0.127
D 0.129

Answer

16. Calculate a working capital ratio for a company financed through current assets of £1.24 million and current liabilities of £310,000. (To calculate a working capital ratio, express this relationship as a ratio in its simplest form.)

A 3 : 1
B 1 : 3
C 4 : 1
D 1 : 4

Answer

17. Divide 15 by 75.

  A 0.1
  B 0.2
  C 0.3
  D 0.4

  ☐ Answer

18. Below are listed the three principal cost elements involved in a production process. Express the relationship as a ratio in its simplest form.

Element	*Cost per unit (in pence)*
Raw materials	3.6
Direct labour	6.0
Factory overheads	2.4

  A 6 : 10 : 4
  B 1 : 3 : 6
  C 3 : 5 : 2
  D 30 : 60 : 24

  ☐ Answer

19. Divide 8 by 12.5.

  A 0.64
  B 0.65
  C 0.66
  D 0.67

  ☐ Answer

20. Calculate the profitability ratio for a product with a net profit margin of 12.5% on total sales of £978,060.

A 87.5 : 1
B 21 : 5
C 7 : 1
D 5 : 1

☐ Answer

21. If a company has current assets of £42,000 and current liabilities of £28,000, what is its working capital ratio (the relationship between current assets and current liabilities)?

A 3 : 2
B 4 : 2
C 5 : 2
D 6 : 2

☐ Answer

22. Divide 3 by 12.

A 0.45
B 0.35
C 0.25
D 0.15

☐ Answer

23. A journal is used to assign a transaction of £462 in the ratio 6 : 8. What is the value of the smaller part of the total?

A £192
B £194
C £196
D £198

☐ Answer

24. Divide 16 by 64.

A 0.25
B 0.30
C 0.35
D 0.40

Answer

25. Calculate the price/earnings ratio for an investment of shares in a limited company if each share has a current market value of 300p and earnings in the current year after corporation tax of 60p.

A 20 : 1
B 15 : 1
C 10 : 1
D 5 : 1

Answer

26. Divide 14 by 80.

A 0.175
B 0.170
C 0.165
D 0.160

Answer

27. Which of the following shares is the most 'expensive' as indicated by its price/earnings ratio?

Share	*market price per share*	*earnings per ordinary share*
A	320p	40p
B	630p	70p
C	500p	50p
D	390p	30p

Answer

Read the two passages and answer the following five questions by writing the answer in the box provided.

Passage 1

One is 40 times more likely to be killed in an accident in the home than in a plane crash, yet safety in the home attracts only a fraction of the money spent on air safety. The chances of dying in an air crash are 1 in 500,000. Such statistics can provide a revealing picture of where money could be used to reduce accidents. Each year 3,900 deaths occur in the home as a result of an accident. Many of these could be prevented if more money was spent on accident prevention in the home.

Passage 2

The Treasury values a life at £1.3 million for use in the cost–benefit calculation as to whether or not a safety improvement is worth the investment. A calculation is made as to how many lives it is believed a safety measure will save and it is multiplied by the Treasury figure for the value of each life; the cost of the measure is then divided by that figure.

In practice, safety schemes seem to be approved using very different cost–benefit figures depending on the mode of transport or location of the accident. Safety schemes are approved for the air industry when the cost per life saved is less than £10 million. Road safety schemes in comparison receive far less funding even though 10 people a day die on our roads. A road safety scheme will fail to be implemented for reasons of cost when the cost per life saved is greater than £100,000. Figures for the cost–benefit intervention point for safety initiatives at home are hard to identify. What evidence there is, however, does suggest that the intervention figure is very low indeed.

28. If it was to cost £37 million to put down new anti-skid surfaces on all the high-speed bends in the road network, what is the minimum number of lives that would be expected to be saved if the proposal was to win approval?

[ ] Answer

29. Use the Treasury value for life figure to calculate the annual cost to the nation of deaths caused by accidents in the home.

Answer

30. What are the chances of dying in an accident in the home?

Answer

31. If safety initiatives could reduce the number of deaths on our roads by 20%, how many lives would be saved in a typical year?

Answer

32. What would be the percentage decrease in the number of deaths caused by accidents in the home if the number of fatalities fell by 234 in a year?

Answer

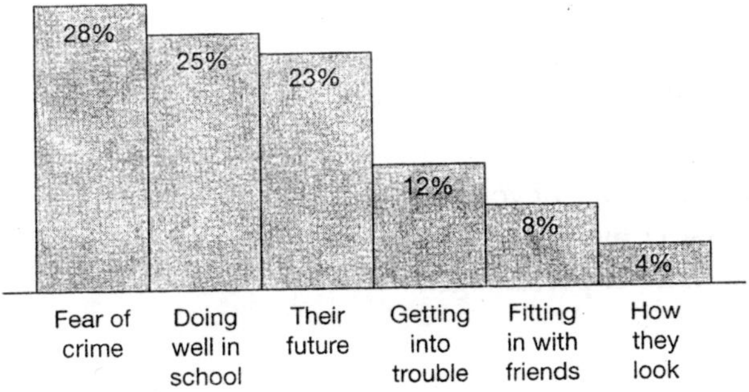

Figure 1 Youth concerns: What concerns 660 young people most

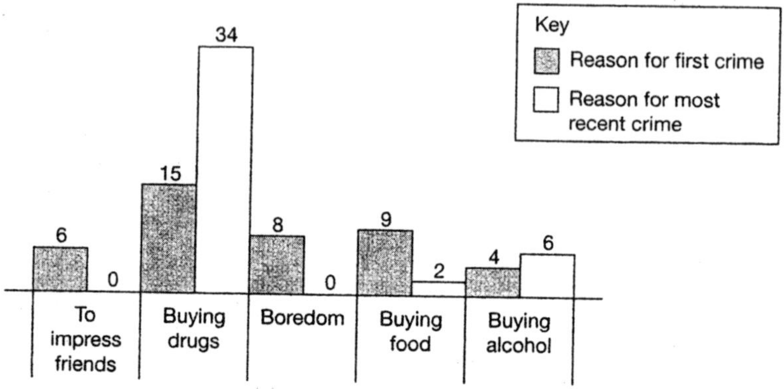

Figure 2 The reason given by 42 young people convicted of more than one crime involving property

33. According to the diagram, how many young people were most concerned with a fear of crime and getting into trouble?

Answer

34. Which reason given for committing a crime saw the greatest percentage increase between the first and most recent crime?

Answer

35. What percentage of young people said that the reason for committing their first crime was boredom? (Express your answer to the nearest whole-number percentage.)

Answer

36. Estimate the ratio between children most concerned with their future or doing well at school compared with those most concerned with getting into trouble.

Answer

37. If in the same survey the previous year there were 30% fewer respondents and doing well in school was stated by 66 of them to be their most pressing concern, what percentage of respondents that year gave this response? (Round your answer up to the nearest whole-number percentage.)

Answer

Manufacturing costs for the production of 50 television (TV) sets	
Direct materials	£1,500
Direct labour	£750
Factory overheads	£3,500
Total factory cost for 50 TV sets	£5,750
Recommended selling price to retailers per set	£128.8

38. From the table, calculate the absorption cost of each TV set (absorption cost = total factory cost divided by the number of units produced).

Answer

39. Calculate the marginal cost of each TV set (marginal cost = direct material and labour cost divided by number of units produced).

Answer

40. What is the percentage profit/loss made on each TV set (use absorption cost in this calculation)?

☐ Answer

41. By how much would total profits increase or fall in relation to the profit made on 50 sets sold at the recommended selling price if 50 more sets were produced (at marginal cost) without incurring any increase in factory overheads and all 100 sets were sold to retailers at £89?

☐ Answer

42. What would the percentage profit be on 50 sets costed at absorption cost and 50 at marginal cost if all 100 sets were sold at £91.20?

☐ Answer

Call Up Telecommunications – latest yearly results, 2005

Group turnover £4.6 bn
Pre-tax profit up £549 m
Earnings per share at 4.8p
Share price £2.64

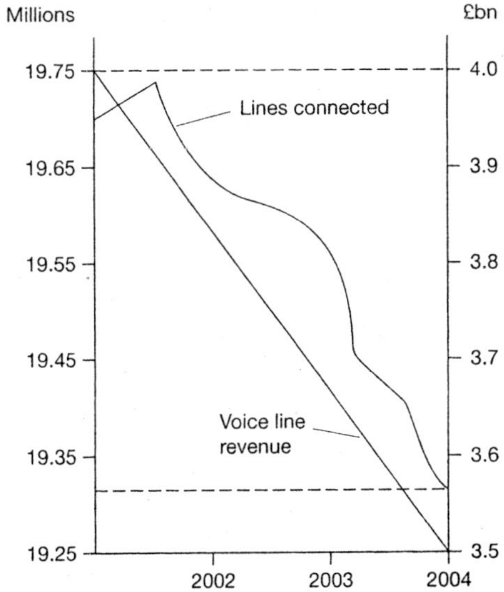

Figure 3 Fixed lines have declined

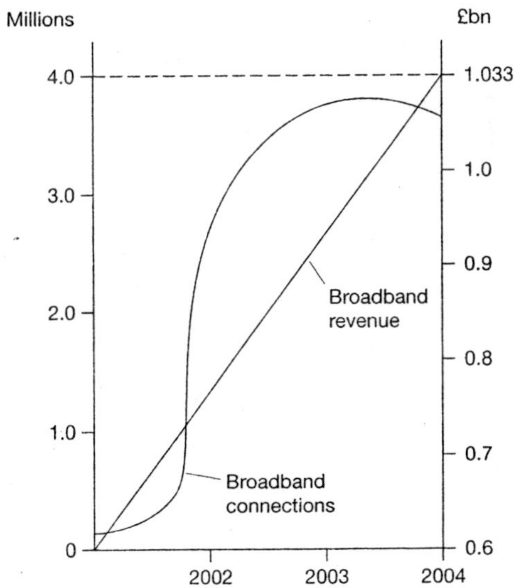

Figure 4 Broadband has soared

43. From the table, what is the price/earnings ratio of shares in Call Up Telecommunications?

☐ Answer

44. At a point in 2002, Call Up Telecommunications provided 19.75 million fixed lines. This figure is projected to fall to 18.96 million. What is this change expressed as a percentage decrease?

☐ Answer

45. From the diagram, how much has broadband services turnover increased from its 2002 figure of £661.12 m? (Express your answer as a percentage.)

☐ Answer

46. If the next year's earnings per share were 4.08p, by what percentage will share earnings have decreased?

☐ Answer

47. What was the net effect on revenue of the decline in fixed line revenue and the increase in broadband revenue over the period covered? (Round your answer to the nearest 0.1£bn.)

The pink and blue candidates election

Most important issue	Cited as main issue	Pink candidate	Blue candidate
Economy	20%	18%	80%
Security	19%	86%	14%
Health	8%	22%	78%
Taxation	5%	56%	44%
Education	4%	25%	75%
No reason given	15%		

Demographic breakdown	Pink	Blue
Men	55%	45%
Women	48%	52%
White	57%	52%
African-Americans	11%	89%
Latino	42%	55%

Education	Pink	Blue
No university degree	52%	47%
University degree	48%	50%

All figures based on exit poll of 5,000 men and 5,000 women.

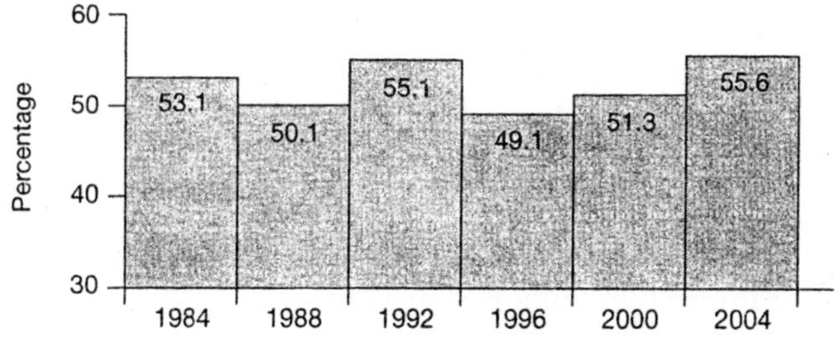

Figure 5 Voter turnout

48. Which election saw the largest percentage decrease in turnout relative to the previous election? (If the question cannot be answered, enter CNT in the answer box.)

Answer

49. What percentage of respondents cited a reason other than those listed for their decision as to how they were to vote?

Answer

50. How many respondents said that they voted for the pink candidate? (If the question cannot be answered, enter CNT in the answer box.)

Answer

51. What is the ratio of support for the pink and blue candidates on the issue of education and tax combined among respondents who cited these issues as their main reason for deciding how they voted? (If the question cannot be answered, enter CNT in the answer box.)

Answer

52. What percentage of all respondents were university graduates? (Record CNT if the question cannot be answered.)

Answer

Customer satisfaction with franchise and independent garages

Twenty-seven per cent of garages were found to be good or very good.
More than two-thirds of garages failed to spot dangerous defects when servicing cars.
A quarter carried out unnecessary work to increase the bill.
Faults were missed by 67%.

These were among the findings of a mystery shopper survey in which 48 cars with known faults were booked in for a service in 48 garages (20 franchises of national chains and 28 independent).

Significant differences in the amount charged were also found. Franchised garages were far more expensive, charging an average of £282 for the same service for which independent garages charged an average of £120.

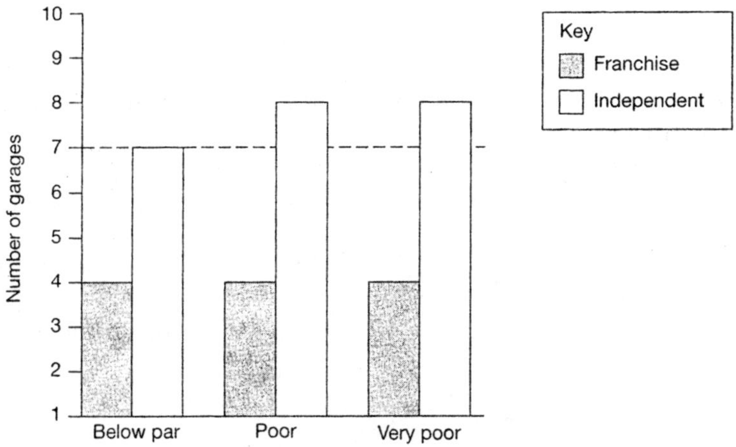

Figure 6 Quality of service

53. How many garages were classed as good or very good?

Answer

54. How many independent garages were classed as below par or worse?

☐ Answer

55. What is the mean amount charged for a service?

☐ Answer

56. What was the ratio of franchised garages classed as very good or good compared with below par or worse?

☐ Answer

57. What is the percentage of franchised garages classed as either below par or worse?

☐ Answer

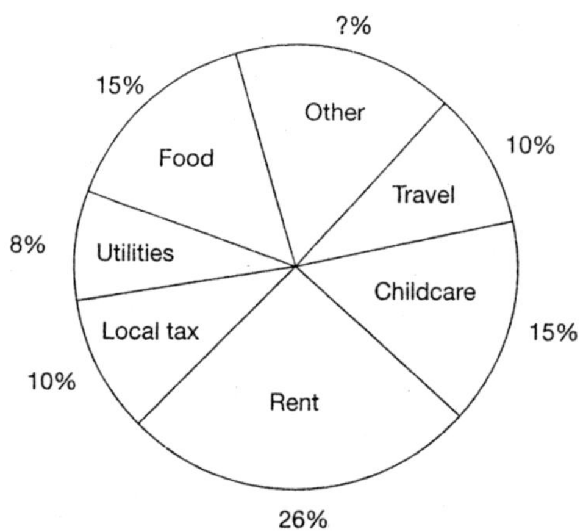

Figure 7 The breakdown of average monthly expenditure for a family

58. From the diagram, what percentage of the family's expenditure is on 'other'?

Answer

59. If the family spends £116 on utilities, how much is the family's total expenditure?

Answer

60. If a flat rate of tax at 25% is paid on all income and the family earns net of tax £1,800, how much is its gross income?

Answer

61. Other expenditure comprises savings, entertainment and luxury items, which are spent in the ratio 3 : 4 : 1. Calculate how much the family saves each month if monthly income is £2,400.

Answer

62. When the eldest child in the family starts school, the family will save 33% of the current childcare expenditure. What is this saving as a percentage change on the monthly total income? (If the question cannot be answered, record CNT in the answer box.)

Answer

Incoming tourism

7% of the UK's total workforce is employed in tourism.
24.4 million overseas visitors came to the UK in 2004.
2004 was a record year for inbound tourism.
This level of visitors was 3% higher than in 2003.
It eclipsed the previous record of 24 million visitors recorded in 1998.
In 2004 while in the UK the average overseas visitor spent £110.

63. How many visitors came to the UK in 2003?

Answer

64. What was the approximate percentage increase on the previous record number of visitors? (Give your answer to 2 sf.)

Answer

65. In total, how much did the inbound tourists contribute to the UK's GDP?

Answer

66. If there are 30 m people employed in the UK workforce, how many work in the tourism sector?

Answer

67. Expenditure by visitors to the UK represents 4% of the UK's total GDP. How much is the total GDP?

Answer

End of test

5

Answers and many detailed explanations

Test 1: Graduate personality questionnaire

1. Interpretation: If you agree with this statement then it may be taken to demonstrate financial acumen. To agree strongly might suggest someone who is risk sensitive. Consider question 69 for consistency of responses.
2. Interpretation: A positive response suggests a confident candidate able to work without supervision. See questions 21, 39, 63 and 84 for consistency.
3. Interpretation: Agreement might suit a candidate for a complex, fast-changing role. Too strong a response could lead an employer to conclude that a candidate risks being over-confident but this would depend on the position. Consider questions 11, 33 and 68 for consistency.
4. Interpretation: A positive response suggests a focused working style; disagreement might suggest a proactive, strategic approach. Consider questions 77, 87 and 93 for consistency.
5. Interpretation: A negative response could be interpreted as a strongly focused or reactive working style. Agreement might suggest a proactive approach. See questions 19, 31 and 45 for consistency.
6. Interpretation: Agreement suggests an eye for detail and a meticulous working style. Consider questions 14, 20, 36 60, 85 and 96 for consistency.

7. Interpretation: Strong agreement would be appropriate if applying for a role that requires the holder to show sensitivity to the needs of others. See questions 18, 32, 44, 52 and 70 for consistency.
8. Interpretation: Agreement suggests a pragmatic approach to work. Disagreement might be expected from a candidate applying to a position that is strategic or involves policy formulation. Consider questions 17 and 46 for consistency.
9. Interpretation: Someone in it for the long term may be more inclined to set procedures and systems that endure and might be expected to agree with this statement. Consider questions 22, 41, 61, 74, 113, 122 and 130 for consistency.
10. Interpretation: Strong agreement suggests suitability for a management role where interpersonal and motivational skills are essential. Strong agreement would not be so important in a role that does not depend on the motivation of others. Consider questions 42, 107, 119 and 126 for consistency.
11. Interpretation: Agreement would suggest a confident approach in a complex or fast-changing environment. Disagreement might suggest a recognition of the importance of strategy and procedures. Consider questions 3, 33 and 68 for consistency.
12. Interpretation: Disagreement would suggest someone best suited to a leadership role that involves policy formation. Agreement might suggest someone with a hands-on, down to earth approach. Consider questions 27, 54, 73 and 94 for consistency.
13. Interpretation: Agreement will suit a networking, client-facing role. Consider questions 51, 82, 110, 121 and 128 for consistency.
14. Interpretation: Agreement suggests a strong eye for detail and high standards of presentation. Strong agreement might not suit an organization that prioritizes results rather than method. See questions 6, 20, 36, 60, 85 and 96 for consistency.
15. Interpretation: Agreement suggests a candidate suitable for a role that requires an ambitious, results-focused person. Consider questions 35, 47, 58, 81, 117 and 125 for consistency.
16. Interpretation: Strong agreement might be expected of a modern thinker in a fast-developing industry. Consider questions 46, 108 and 114 for consistency.

17. Interpretation: Many organizations state that the post holder will be pragmatic, and agreement with this statement would suggest that attribute. Consider questions 8 and 46 for consistency.
18. Interpretation: Some industries might expect strong agreement while others might prefer agreement but not strong. For example, a role that requires the post holder to show sensitivity to others might best suit a strong response.
19. Interpretation: A positive response suggests a proactive or risk-sensitive approach to work. Consider questions 5, 35, 45, 71, 62 and 100 for consistency of answer.
20. Interpretation: Agreement suggests a numerate applicant.
21. Interpretation: Agreement suggests suitability to a role that involves working without daily supervision. See questions 2, 39, 63 and 84 for consistency.
22. Interpretation: Strong agreement would suggest a safe pair of hands. Consider questions 9, 41, 61, 74, 113, 122 and 130.
23. Interpretation: Agreement would suggest a manager or leader who relied on inspiration and charisma. Consider questions 49 and 106 for consistency.
24. Interpretation: Agreement suggests a motivated, hands-on manager, and some employers are looking for exactly that. Consider questions 50 and105 for consistency.
25. Interpretation: Agreement might suggest a candidate suitable for a role in which they must operate as an agent for change. See questions 67 and 104 for consistency.
26. Interpretation: Agreement suggests a candidate suitable for a customer-facing role and a sales-orientated, ambitious candidate. Consider questions 82, 110 and 121 for consistency.
27. Interpretation: Agreement suggests a need to know the bigger picture and to be involved in policy. See questions 12, 54, 73 and 94 for consistency.
28. Interpretation: Strong agreement would suggest a mature (in the non-ageist sense) approach and a candidate who would represent a safe pair of hands. If this is a part of your character that you wish to emphasize then see questions 57, 78, 115 and 118 for consistency.
29. Interpretation: Agreement suggests a candidate well suited for a team role. See questions 102, 109, 116 and 123 for consistency.

30. Interpretation: Agreement would support a candidate for a role in an organization that required independence but otherwise it could suggest a candidate who would find it difficult to fit most teams. See questions 38, 76 and 91 for consistency.
31. Interpretation: Agreement suggests a strong preference for working proactively. See questions 5, 19 and 45 for consistency.
32. Interpretation: Strong agreement suggests an applicant capable of being sensitive to the needs of others. See questions 7, 18, 44, 52 and 70 for consistency.
33. Interpretation: Disagreement would suggest a candidate suitable for working in a fast-changing, complex role. See questions 3, 11 and 68 for consistency.
34. Interpretation: Strong agreement would suggest a preference for a professional role within an organization. See questions 48, 53, 66 and 99 for consistency.
35. Interpretation: Agreement will suggest an ambitious candidate determined to make an impression. It will appeal to some employers but might put others off. Consider questions 15, 47, 58, 81, 117 and 125 for consistency.
36. Interpretation: Strong agreement suggests someone who works in a meticulous style and values accuracy. See questions 6, 14, 20, 60, 85 and 96 for consistency.
37. Interpretation: Strong agreement might suggest suitability for a performance-oriented role. Consider questions 90 and 92 for consistency.
38. Interpretation: Agreement would be appropriate for a candidate applying for a role that required the provision of independent advice. See questions 30, 76 and 91 for consistency.
39. Interpretation: Essential to agree if applying to many graduate roles, especially if they involve working independently of a supervisor or manager. Consider questions 2, 21, 63 and 84 for consistency.
40. Interpretation: A negative response may indicate someone who is strongly sales orientated, a change facilitator or suitable for a role where the status quo has to be challenged. See questions 1, 71 and 100 for consistency of response.

41. Interpretation: Strong agreement suggests an uncompromising commitment to procedure. Consider questions 9, 22, 74, 113, 122 and 130 for consistency.
42. Interpretation: Some organizations will value a strong commitment to this motivational approach. Consider questions 10, 107, 119 and 126 for consistency.
43. Interpretation: Unless you are applying to work as an electrician or handy person, agreement might imply an approach best suited to a hierarchical place of work and a degree of inflexibility.
44. Interpretation: In some roles and industries this is the only acceptable approach and if you are applying to such an area then you must reflect that culture in your answers. See questions 7, 18, 32, 52 and 70 for consistency.
45. Interpretation: Strong agreement indicates a proactive, wide-view approach; a negative response may suggest a focused, reactive approach. For consistency of answer consider questions 31, 19 and 5.
46. Interpretation: A modern thinker and dynamic business developer would agree strongly with this statement. See questions 16, 108 and 114 for consistency.
47. Interpretation: Disagreement would suggest a team player, agreement an ambitious, performance-oriented candidate. For consistency on the issue of ambition see questions 15, 35, 58, 81, 117 and 125.
48. Interpretation: Agreement strongly suggests a professional and independent role within an organization. See questions 34, 53, 66 and 99 for consistency.
49. Interpretation: Agreement implies an inspirational style of management or leadership. Consider questions 23 and 106 for consistency.
50. Interpretation: Agreement implies a very hands-on approach to management and perhaps strong agreement would suggest a lack of trust in colleagues.
51. Interpretation: This quality is relevant to internal management as well as networking-relationship-type customer-facing roles. In the latter case consider questions 13, 26, 82, 110, 121 and 128 for consistency.
52. Interpretation: A negative response would suit a role in which the post holder must show sensitivity to the needs of others but in some

roles a positive response may be seen as a virtue. See questions 7, 18, 32, 44, and 70 for consistency.

53. Interpretation: A positive response is relevant to a professional and/or leadership role. Some organizations might find strong agreement to imply a candidate who might not fit well into an existing team. See questions 34, 48, 66 and 99 for consistency.
54. Interpretation: Agreement suggests a policy formulator or someone who prefers a workplace with procedures. See questions 12, 27, 73 and 94 for consistency.
55. Interpretation: Agreement suggests an entrepreneur who might be well suited for a business development position. See questions 103, 112, 120 and 129 for consistency.
56. Interpretation: Agreement will suggest a candidate suitable for a sales-orientated role. See questions 101, 111, 124 and 127 for consistency.
57. Interpretation: Strong agreement would suggest a mature approach and a safe pair of hands. See questions 28, 78, 115 and 118 for consistency.
58. Interpretation: Agreement suggests an ambitious candidate with considerable confidence in his or her potential. It might be most appropriate to agree with this statement if you are applying for a commission-based role.
59. Interpretation: Agreement might suggest someone who sees themselves as an all-rounder. See questions 72, 79, 88 and 97 for consistency.
60. Interpretation: Agreement suggests a meticulous approach and an eye for detail. See questions 6, 14, 20, 36, 85 and 96 for consistency.
61. Interpretation: A strong response suggests an independent, uncompromising, reliable candidate. See questions 9, 22, 41, 74, 113, 122 and 130 for consistency.
62. Interpretation: Agreement may indicate a preference for a financial position and someone risk sensitive. See questions 40, 71 and 100 for consistency.
63. Interpretation: If the role for which you are applying involves working without supervision then only a strong positive response would be acceptable. See questions 2, 21, 39, 43 and 84 for consistency.
64. Interpretation: Strong agreement suggests a reactive style. Some businesses are seeking highly reactive staff but make sure you are

applying to such an organization before you stress this side of your personality. See questions 75, 83, 89 and 98 for consistency.

65. Interpretation: Agreement suggests a pragmatic approach to work. See questions 8, 17 and 46 for consistency.
66. Interpretation: A positive response suggests a professional approach. See questions 34, 48, 53 and 99 for consistency.
67. Interpretation: Agreement suggests someone suitable for a role as an agent of change. See questions 25 and 104 for consistency.
68. Interpretation: Agreement might suggest that the person would excel in complex and fast-changing environments. A negative response might be preferred by an organization operating in a rule-bound, regulatory environment. See questions 3, 11 and 33 for consistency.
69. Interpretation: This side is concerned with trade accounts payable, debts and equity. A positive response shows financial acumen; a strong response shows preference for financial positions. See question 1 for consistency of response.
70. Interpretation: Agreement may be an appropriate response for some roles but a negative response would be required in any that requires sensitivity to the needs of others. See questions 7, 18, 32, 44 and 52 for consistency.
71. Interpretation: A positive response may indicate a person who is risk sensitive and suited to a role where a counterbalance to a strong sales ethos is required. See questions 1, 40 and 100 for consistency.
72. Interpretation: Agreement suggests a candidate suitable for an all-rounder type of role; disagreement might suggest someone more suited for a role that demands focus. See questions 59, 79, 88 and 97 for consistency.
73. Interpretation: Strong agreement suggests a candidate with a preference for policy and its formulation. See questions 12, 27, 54 and 94 for consistency.
74. Interpretation: Strong agreement suggests a very reliable person who can be trusted to get on with a task. See questions 9, 22, 41, 61, 113, 122 and 130 for consistency.
75. Interpretation: Agreement suggests a reactive style of management. See questions 64, 83, 89 and 98 for consistency.

76. Interpretation: Agreement would suggest a strongly independent approach and might suit some professional roles. See questions 30, 38 and 91 for consistency.
77. Interpretation: A positive response suggests a focused style of working. See questions 4, 87 and 93 for consistency.
78. Interpretation: Strong agreement might appeal to an employer looking for a mature approach in a candidate. Consider questions 28, 57, 115 and 118 for consistency.
79. Interpretation: Strong agreement would suggest someone suitable for another position that is highly flexible and broad. See questions 59, 72, 88 and 97 for consistency.
80. Interpretation: Agreement might suggest someone who is not a team player. See questions 29, 102, 109 and 123 for consistency on that issue; see also questions 107, 115, 119 and 126.
81. Interpretation: Agreement would suggest an ambitious candidate who placed great emphasis on performance. For consistency consider questions 15, 35, 47, 58, 117 and 125.
82. Interpretation: Agreement supports a candidate as suitable for a client-networking role. Consider questions 13, 26, 51, 110, 121 and 128 for consistency.
83. Interpretation: A strong response risks implying a certain lack of foresight; however, it would also suggest a very reactive style, which is by no means necessarily a bad thing. See questions 64, 75, 89 and 98 for consistency.
84. Interpretation: A negative response would better suit someone in a role where they had responsibility or worked unsupervised. A better response would involve reporting the problem immediately while working to put it right. For consistency of answer see questions 2, 21, 39, 43 and 63.
85. Interpretation: Agreement implies an eye for detail and an uncompromising approach to accuracy. See questions 6, 14, 20, 36, 60 and 96 for consistency.
86. Interpretation: Few employers would want in a position of responsibility someone who agreed with this statement. When the news is bad, report it straight away, taking the opportunity to explain what is being done to correct it.

87. Interpretation: Disagreement might support the view that the candidate is more strategic a policy formulator, perhaps. Agreement suggests a focused work style. See questions 4, 77 and 93 for consistency.
88. Interpretation: A positive response suggests a person suited to an all-rounder type of position. See questions 59, 72, 79 and 97 for consistency.
89. Interpretation: Agreement suggests that success in business requires a reactive approach. See questions 64, 75, 83 and 98 for consistency.
90. Interpretation: Strong agreement might be expected of a candidate for a commission-based, target-driven role. See questions 37 and 92 for consistency.
91. Interpretation: Strong agreement would suit an independent role or professional position within an organization. See questions 30, 38 and 76 for consistency.
92. Interpretation: Strong disagreement might indicate a preference for performance-orientated roles. See questions 37 and 90 for consistency.
93. Interpretation: Disagreement might suggest a candidate sensitive to the needs of others; a positive response might suggest someone highly focused and driven. See questions 4, 77 and 87 for consistency.
94. Interpretation: Agreement suggests a candidate best suited for a role that affords strategic awareness. See questions 12, 27, 54 and 73 for consistency.
95. Interpretation: Agreement might suggest a candidate who is hard to manage.
96. Interpretation: Agreement suggests a hands-on management style and a liking for detail. See questions 6, 14, 20, 60 and 85 for consistency.
97. Interpretation: Some employers are looking for flexible, multitasked staff; others prefer specialists. A positive response would suggest the candidate is an all-rounder while a more negative response would imply a person better suited for a task-defined role. See questions 59, 72, 79 and 88 for consistency.
98. Interpretation: Strong agreement might suggest a lack of foresight and a highly reactive style. For some positions a reactive style is exactly what is being looked for. See questions 64, 75, 83 and 89.
99. Interpretation: A strong response would suggest a professional role or one where the candidate is required to bring stature. See questions 34, 48, 53 and 66.

100. Interpretation: A positive response may indicate someone who is risk sensitive; a strongly negative response may indicate someone who is sales driven or a change facilitator. See questions 1, 40 and 71 for consistency of answer.
101. Interpretation: Agreement suggests a candidate well suited to sales positions. Consider questions 56, 111, 124 and 127 for consistency.
102. Interpretation: Agreement suggests people skills and suitability for a team-player role. Consider questions 29, 109, 116 and 123 for consistency.
103. Interpretation: Strong agreement should be supported by your CV and indicates an entrepreneur. Consider questions 55, 112, 120 and 129 for consistency.
104. Interpretation: This is a well-known analogy for entirely changing a business without interrupting trade. Agreement would therefore suggest a candidate suitable for a role of agent of change. See questions 25 and 67 for consistency.
105. Interpretation: Strong agreement would suggest a hands-on leadership or management style. See questions 50 and 24 for consistency.
106. Interpretation: Agreement would suggest a candidate suitable for a leadership role where an inspirational style was sought. See questions 23 and 49 for consistency.
107. Interpretation: Strong agreement suggests preference for a style of team motivation and management preferred by some organizations. Consider questions 10, 42, 119 and 126 for consistency.
108. Interpretation: Strong agreement would be evidence of a flexibility of mind and working approach that some employers value highly. See questions 16, 48 and 114 for consistency.
109. Interpretation: Strong agreement will support the view that a candidate is sensitive to the needs of colleagues and a team player. Consider questions 29, 102, 116 and 123 for consistency.
110. Interpretation: A negative response will strongly suggest that you are better suited to back-office roles. If you agreed with the statement then consider questions 13, 26, 51, 82, 121 and 128 for consistency.
111. Interpretation: Agreement indicates a strong sales orientation in the candidate. See questions 56, 101, 124 and 127 for consistency.

112. Interpretation: Agreement would mean that the candidate had proven influencing skills and an aptitude for business development. See for consistency questions 55, 103, 120 and 129.
113. Interpretation: Agreement suggests someone who can be relied on to continue the operation of a successful formula rather than shape the future. See questions 9, 22, 41, 61, 74, 122 and 130 for consistency.
114. Interpretation: A candidate with an open mind and flexible working style might agree with this statement. See questions 16, 46 and 108 for consistency.
115. Interpretation: Agreement would need to be supported by a CV and it would suggest a low-risk appointment.
116. Interpretation: Agreement suggests a team player. See questions 29, 102, 109 and 123 for consistency.
117. Interpretation: Agreement suggests an ambitious, determined individual who will suit the culture of some organizations but not all. Consider questions 15, 35, 47, 58, 81 and 125 for consistency.
118. Interpretation: Disagreement suggests a candidate that may come over as a little cynical.
119. Interpretation: Strong agreement suggests a team player who can lead a motivated group in a no-blame culture. Consider questions 42, 107 and 126 for consistency.
120. Interpretation: An entrepreneur and candidate suitable for a business development role would agree with this statement. See questions 55, 103, 112 and 129 for consistency.
121. Interpretation: Strong agreement suggests a networking or similar role. Consider questions 13, 26, 51, 82, 110 and 128 for consistency.
122. Interpretation: Agreement suggests a safe pair of hands that will keep things steady. See questions 9, 22, 41, 61, 74, 113, 130 for consistency.
123. Interpretation: Agreement suggests a non-confrontational approach to work and a strong team player. Consider questions 29, 102, 109 and 126 for consistency.
124. Interpretation: Agreement suggests an ambitious sales-orientated candidate. See questions 56, 101, 111 and 127 for consistency.

125. Interpretation: Agreement demonstrates ambition and self-belief – qualities of yours worth stressing if that is what the organization is looking for. Consider questions 15, 35, 47, 58, 81 and 117 for consistency.
126. Interpretation: Strong agreement suggests a candidate who knows the value of motivating others. Consider questions 10, 42, 107 and 119 for consistency.
127. Interpretation: Strong agreement might suggest a confident, ambitious, sales-orientated person. See questions 56, 101, 111 and 124 for consistency.
128. Interpretation: Agreement suggests suitability for a client-facing networking role. Consider questions 13, 26, 51, 82, 110 and 121 for consistency.
129. Interpretation: Agreement suggests a willingness to take risks and perhaps an entrepreneurial style. Consider questions 55, 103, 112 and 120 for consistency.
130. Interpretation: If you agree strongly then you are telling an employer that you are a safe pair of hands. See questions 9, 22, 41, 61, 74, 113 and 122 for consistency.

Test 2: Analysis of information

1. A, True

   The passage states that existing fuels should be made to go further.

2. B, False

   It is stated that substantial avoidable waste also occurs in factories and to a lesser extent transport. It is false therefore to conclude that the opportunity exists mainly in the domestic sector.

3. C, Cannot tell

   The passage recommends greater effort but it does not comment on whether that effort will be made.

4. A, True
   This can be inferred from the passage, as it reports that the market has since dipped.

5. C, Cannot tell
   Profits were reported at 50% ahead. The passage states that the average selling price was strongly ahead but no percentage is given, nor can it be inferred.

6. B, False
   The passage states that consumer confidence has dropped and from this we can infer that they are less optimistic.

7. B, False
   Girls are more prone by a ratio of 3 to 1.

8. C, Cannot tell
   This information is not contained in the passage and cannot be inferred from the passage.

9. A, True
   It is stated in the passage that the higher incidence of infestation among girls is related to the fact that their play involves longer periods of head contact. From this we can infer that prolonged contact of heads can lead to a child contracting head lice.

10. A, True
    The passage states that given the shortage these central banks have decided they have no alternative but to withdraw the coins.

11. C, Cannot tell
    The passage does not state whether or not there is a shortage in France. There may well be such a shortage; however, that there is a shortage cannot be inferred from the passage.

12. B, False
    The one- and two-cent coins will remain in circulation at least in France.

13. A, True
    This point is clearly stated in the passage.

14. C, Cannot tell
    The passage only reports on a fall in the level of homelessness in London. The experience for Britain as a whole cannot be inferred.

15. B, False
    The passage notes differences between the cities but no case is made as to why a comparison between the cities is reasonable.

16. A, True
    The statement's truth follows from the fact stated that the vast majority of respondents in the survey were opposed to the extension. It can therefore be expected that the opposition may continue.

17. A, True
    The passage states that the zone is to be extended to these thickly populated areas in which many people will qualify for residential discounts.

18. B, False
    Residents of the extended area will become eligible for the residents' discount and this risks a potential revenue drop for the scheme. From this it can be inferred that they currently have to pay the full charge.

19. A, True
    While the passage does not report the respondents' view on these matters, it is possible that they were of this view.

20. A, True
    The passage states that there have been four successive increases.

21. C, Cannot tell
    We are told that the cost since 1997 has more than doubled and that the bill in some towns has risen by more than £10,000. But from this we cannot infer the cost of this tax on a house purchased that year.

22. B, False
    The passage states that the highest band of 4% applies to properties over half a million, and the percentage figure for the lower band, while not given, will be lower than 4%.

23. C, Cannot tell
    The cost of controlling the current plague is not stated and cannot be inferred from the passage.

24. B, False
    The passage does not state that donors have been asked to provide $15 million; this figure relates to the amount released by the United Nations to assist eradication.

25. A, True
    The passage states that last month hundreds of swarms were reported and crops devastated. The ground when stripped of everything green is also sown with eggs that hatch after 30 days. It is true, therefore, that the next generation of locusts is due to hatch.

26. B, False
    It asserts a fact that could be tested.

27. B, False
    While Spanish-speaking Americans are now the largest ethnic minority group, that does not mean that Spanish is the most widely spoken minority language.

28. C, Cannot tell
    The size of the Latino population in relation to the overall population of the United States is not detailed in the passage and cannot be inferred from it.

29. C, Cannot tell
    This information is neither provided nor can it be inferred.

30. B, False
    The growth is due mainly to this but also the passing of the SARS crisis.

31. A, True
    The economy is 12.5% higher this year than in the same period last year.

32. A, True
    The passage describes the United States as the only industrialized nation due to experience significant population growth.

33. A, True
    Britain is described as an industrialized nation and the United States as the only industrialized nation that will experience significant growth.

34. C, Cannot tell
    The passage only provides information on the relative population sizes in 25 years' time. No information is provided about the current relative sizes. We cannot, then, infer the truth or falsehood of the statement.

35. A, True
    This statement's truth is implied by the content of the passage. All stations could receive the information at the same time, either early or when the markets open.

36. B, False
    Information about audience numbers is share-price sensitive and the share value may go either up or down whatever the change in audience levels. It is false, therefore, that the share price will go down as it is possible that it will rise if, for example, the drop in audience is less than the market had already adjusted for.

37. B, False
    The passage contains statements in support of both the status quo (where public channels receive the information 12 hours before commercial stations) and the early release of the information to both types of station.

38. A, True
    A flash flood occurs when heavy rain falls over geographic features such as steep-sided valleys.

39. C, Cannot tell
    A downpour of 50 millimetres over a kilometre is described as not rare. The frequency of a downpour of 15 centimetres is not quantified and cannot be inferred from the passage.

40. B, False
    The passage states that flash floods are associated with downpours of rain over certain geographic features. This implies that it is in fact possible to predict where they might occur.

41. B, False
    They are attributed to record demand in both new and mature markets.

42. B, False
    The 700 million forecast is for sales next year, which will be six years after sales of 200 million were realized.

43. B, False
This year's forecast has been increased three times by a total of almost 100 million so the most recent increase could not have been for the full amount.

44. C, Cannot tell
The number of people against the proposal is not detailed and cannot be inferred.

45. B, False
The proposal is to clone the lions and the argument against this (so the counter-argument) is made in some detail.

46. B, False
The passage does not state this. It reports the views of the scientists on the role of biotechnological intervention.

47. A, True
This can be inferred from the passage as the plan would not risk breaking EU legislation otherwise.

48. B, False
The conflict might exist over the transfer of personal details, not jobs.

49. A, True
The passage states that details cannot be transferred without written consent, therefore the truth of this statement can be inferred from the passage.

50. A, True
The chances have increased from 27,500 to 24,000 to one; the number of winning numbers has increased because of this improvement in odds and also because there are more numbers in the draw.

51. B, False
    The new machine completes the task in half the previous five and a half hours; this means that the draw now takes 165 minutes.

52. C, Cannot tell
    The construction of the new machine is not detailed and cannot be inferred from the passage.

53. B, False
    Self-discipline is described as critical but the passage does not suggest that a foundation degree student must show more self-discipline than a conventional degree student.

54. B, False
    The opening sentence makes it clear that doing a foundation degree involves going to university.

55. B, False
    It is also suggested that the foundation degree student is better able to compete for graduate-level jobs because of their relevant work experience.

56. B, False
    This is not the necessary outcome; they may, for example, have long-term contracts with suppliers that protect them from the commodity price rises.

57. A, True
    Until they are able to pass on the price increases, manufacturers' margins will be eroded.

58. B, False
    The passage also identifies emission trading and climate control as further sources of pressure and does not indicate which if any represents the more serious challenge.

59. A, True
The free movement of people to the United States a hundred years ago is contrasted to the barriers to such movement today.

60. B, False
Governments must ensure that their economies are competitive because of the relative free movement of capital, not because of the restrictions on the movement of labour.

61. B, False
Globalization is described as a situation where factories and capital migrate. If workers were also able to move around the world then the process would be more, not less, pronounced.

62. A, True
To be discriminatory is to be unequal in your treatment on the basis of prejudice. Therefore the government and media sanction discrimination by repeating the view that young teenage mothers are irresponsible burdens on the state.

63. B, False
They are described as found in government and the media but they are not described in the passage as prevalent.

64. C, Cannot tell.
This specific claim is not reported and it cannot be inferred from the passage.

65. B, False
Cold weather is described as causing the blood to thicken and possibly clot, not hypertension.

66. B, False
They have a 60% greater risk of a heart attack, not a 60% risk.

67. C, Cannot tell
The relationship between hypertension and heart attacks is linked to a rapid drop in temperature and not to particular months or seasons.

Test 3: Analysis of information

1. C, Cannot tell
Most flag carriers have raised a surcharge on short-haul passengers. No information is provided on the policy towards long-haul passengers and the answer cannot be inferred from the passage.

2. A, True
The passage states that national carriers have reduced fares on their short-haul European operations.

3. B, False
Losses have not occurred on short-haul flights. The passage states that no money will be made on these operations.

4. B, False
Traders have noticed that some countries are purchasing stock at levels above their rate of consumption.

5. A, True
The truth of the statement is a valid inference.

6. C, Cannot tell
Traders have recently increased the level of world demand but no information is given as to when these countries became major oil importers and this information cannot be inferred from the passage.

7. B, False
The assertion is not made, nor can it be inferred. The result can be explained otherwise; it could be, for example, due to bias in the test.

8. A, True
   This can be inferred from the opening statements of the passage.

9. B, False
   Satire is a mocking, jocular style with a sharp critical edge of someone or something.

10. B, False
    They are almost as economical but hybrid-powered cars have the environmental advantage that emissions are far lower than for diesel-powered cars.

11. A, True
    An economic case could be made for very high-mileage drivers in the United States but not in Europe. This is because the option to buy a diesel-powered car is open to such European drivers but not their US counterparts.

12. B, False
    The higher initial cost of hybrids means a longer payback time the further fuel costs drop and so a weaker economic case.

13. C, Cannot tell
    Eighty per cent is a high percentage of most things but we do not know what the reuse rate is for other things so cannot make a relative judgement.

14. C, Cannot tell
    These points are not made in the passage and do not follow from its content.

15. B, False
    The passage would contribute to both sides of such a debate.

16. A, True
Students find it easier to obtain top marks now that course work and projects are awarded marks that count towards the final grade.

17. C, Cannot tell
We cannot tell whether the statement is true or false because the total number of A grades awarded is not given.

18. B, False
Because the number of A grades has more than doubled from the previous 10% of candidates, the proportion of students who now score over 60% must be more than 20%.

19. B, False
The case includes the fact of the growing number of cases in industrial tribunals.

20. A, True
This further example is consistent with those given in the passage and so would serve to further illustrate the point made.

21. A, True
The number of claims for compensation (excluding those in industrial tribunals) is falling, so we do not face a higher risk of a claim outside of employment.

22. A, True
These sectors are identified in the passage as among the big spenders who suffered the effects.

23. A, True
Other reasons might exist for holding cash but the passage gives examples that suggest a cautious outlook is one. It is therefore reasonable to conclude from the passage that cash at hand is a symptom of such an approach.

24. B, False

    The passage states that this is a mistake made in the 1990s but it does not imply that, in general, over-investment leads to excessive production capacity.

25. C, Cannot tell

    No information is provided on the emotional state of the caged cod and this information cannot be inferred from the passage.

26. A, True

    The cod farmers are implementing measures that aim to address the reasons for the discrediting of salmon farming.

27. A, True

    The passage states that cod farmers have adopted rules for fish welfare.

28. A, True

    The waste from nuclear power is its major drawback. Solving it would give it a strong environmental case.

29. A, True

    The passage describes the visual intrusion caused by renewable sources.

30. C, Cannot tell

    The passage does not provide this information and it cannot be inferred.

31. A, True

    The issues are laundering and tax avoidance, and on the issue of laundering the rules do seem to be different currently.

32. B, False

    They will be required to provide information only on clients they suspect of money laundering or tax avoidance.

33. C, Cannot tell
    Whether or not this is a motive of the accountants is not covered in the passage and cannot be inferred from it.

34. C, Cannot tell
    This issue is not discussed in the passage and cannot be inferred.

35. B, False
    Twenty-seven per cent of UK jobs are advertised on the net.

36. A, True
    The passage states that one of the most commonly cited reasons for advertising jobs on the net was cost-effectiveness.

37. A, True
    It is reported that the vast majority of employers do not consider it a significant issue, and evidence of a detrimental impact at work is hard to find.

38. B, False
    There is a potential conflict on the issue of testing staff for the use of recreational drugs in order to provide a safe workplace in some critical industries.

39. C, Cannot tell
    The passage does not comment on this issue, and the truth or otherwise of the statement cannot be inferred from the passage.

40. A, True
    Had the technologies that gave rise to these problems been assessed before being implemented then these problems might have been avoided.

41. B, False
    The benefits would not be realized unless most governments adopted the recommendation.

42. C, Cannot tell
    The passage does not provide this information and it cannot be inferred from the passage.

43. A, True
    The condition is activated by a chaotic or difficult home environment.

44. B, False
    While this many children are at risk of suffering the condition, it cannot be inferred that they all share this type of experience at home.

45. B, False
    The passage states that this is only the case if the condition is left untreated.

46. C, Cannot tell
    The passage is concerned with the price of homes in the capital relative to the rest of the UK over the past five years. The cost of homes in real terms over this period is not covered and cannot be inferred.

47. A, True
    The passage predicts that the current trend will be reversed, given the number of people wanting to move into the city over the next two decades.

48. A, True
    The divide will widen as house prices in the capital rise faster than prices in the rest of the country.

49. C, Cannot tell
    Something that is carcinogenic can cause cancer. Contradictory information is provided on whether or not a compound of nitrates can cause cancer, so it is not possible to decide whether this is true or not.

50. A, True
    The passage states that a great many studies have failed to find such a link.

51. A, True
    This is the new, positive view of dietary nitrates described in the passage.

52. B, False
    No compulsory element is described.

53. B, False
    The initiative is offered to employees who have medical insurance paid for by their employers.

54. A, True
    This is an example of the kind of intervention that could be offered under the initiative.

55. A, True
    The most efficient experimental hydrogen car is less efficient than the best production car with a diesel combustion engine and, if widely adopted, hydrogen risks greater environmental damage.

56. B, False
    The environmental impact of the hydrogen economy could be worse or better than the petroleum economy but it is false to say that it would be worse.

57. B, False
    The passage predicts that such a powered car will become a reality but it is not supportive (or critical) of that development.

58. A, True
    The study reports on trends in mental health over 25 years.

59. A, True
The conditions are reported across social class and racial groups and affect members of all family types as well as girls and boys.

60. B, False
A number of possible causes are considered and rejected such as inequality or the rise in the frequency of single parents.

61. A, True
If the theory is correct then this is a local extension of it.

62. B, False
It could also mean that the population is elderly but its members have not yet made significant drawings from their savings.

63. A, True
Again this is a logical prediction from the theory.

64. B, False
Eight flight tests have taken place but the test programme has included simulations and theoretical models in addition to these.

65. A, True
It is stated that a lot of the development programme has relied on models and simulations.

66. C, Cannot tell.
The passage does not contain this information, nor can it be inferred.

Test 4: Data interpretation

1. 16.5
   $30 \div 100 \times 55$

2. 9.6
   $80 \div 100 \times 12$

3. 22.5
   $5 \div 100 \times 450$

4. 2.55
   $17 \div 100 \times 15$

5. 38.5
   $22 \div 100 \times 175$

6. 22.8
   $38 \div 100 \times 60$

7. 24.2
   $11 \div 100 \times 220$

8. 432
   $90 \div 100 \times 480$

9. 42.75
   $57 \div 100 \times 75$

10. 266.4
    $74 \div 100 \times 360$

11. 58.8
    $60 \div 100 \times 98$

12. 75.9
    $23 \div 100 \times 330$

13. 0.28
    $56 \div 100 \times 0.5$

14. 40.6
    $7 \div 100 \times 580$

15. 32.4
    $36 \div 100 \times 90$

16. 9.1
    $13 \div 100 \times 70$

17. 65.6
    $41 \div 100 \times 160$

18. 6.3
    $14 \div 100 \times 45$

19. 70.56
    $84 \div 100 \times 84$

20. 2%
    100% = 2,500p, 1% = 25p, $2 \times 25 = 50$

21. 5%
    100% = 2,000 ml, 1% = 20 ml, $5 \times 20 = 100$

22. 5%
    2 hours = 120 minutes so 100% = 120, 1% = 1.2, $5 \times 1.2 = 6$

23. 0.05%
    1 km = 1,000 metres and 500 cm = 0.5 of a metre. 100% = 1,000, 1% = 0.1 and $0.5 \times 0.1 = 0.05$%

24. 0.25%
 £1 = 1%. 25p as a percentage of 100p = 0.25

25. 12.5%
 26 weeks is 50% of one year so 12.5% of four

26. 2.25%

27. 1.25%

28. 6.25%

29. 0.4%

30. 1.5%

31. 0.5%
 1 hour 40 minutes = $60 \times 60 = 3{,}600$, $40 \times 60 = 2{,}400$ = 6,000 seconds.
 30 as percentage of 6,000 = 1 in 200 = 0.5%

32. 3.33%
 12 metres = 12,000 mm, 400 as a percentage of 12,000 = 4, as a percentage of 120 = 1, as a percentage of 30 = 3.33%

33. 14%
 1.2 kilometres = 1,200 metres, 1% = 12, $12 \times 14 = 168$

34. 2%
 365 days =100%, 1% = 3.65, $7.3 \div 3.65 = 2$

35. 4%
 100% = 4500p, 1% = 45p, $180 = 4 \times 45$

36. 22.5%
 $45 \div 200 \times 100$

37. 90%
 $630 \div 700 \times 100$

38. 25%
 $31.5 \div 126 \times 100$

39. 6%
 $5.4 \div 90 \times 100$

40. 33.33%
 $32 \div 96 \times 100$

41. 32%
 $144 \div 450 \times 100$

42. 45%
 $135 \div 300 \times 100$

43. 20%
 $72 \div 360 \times 100$

44. 17%
 $42.5 \div 250 \times 100$

45. 35%
 $665 \div 1{,}900 \times 100$

46. 16.7%
 $10 \div 60 \times 100$

47. 15%
 $21 \div 140 \times 100$

48. 85%
 $17 \div 20 \times 100$

49. 37.5%
   $24 \div 64 \times 100$

50. 27.5%
   $11 \div 40 \times 100$

51. 80%
   $360 \div 450 \times 100$

52. 41.25%
   $165 \div 400 \times 100$

53. 48%
   $120 \div 250 \times 100$

54. 75%
   $1{,}200 \div 1{,}600 \times 100$

55. 24%
   $19.2 \div 80 \times 100$

56. 25%
   Percentage decrease = decrease divided by the initial value × 100 = $2 \div 8 \times 100 = 25$

57. 30%
   Percentage increase = increase divided by initial value × 100 = $18 \div 60 \times 100 = 30$

58. 60%
   $42 \div 70 = 0.6 \times 100 = 60$

59. 16%
   $12 \div 75 = 0.16 \times 100 = 16$

60. 20%
   $3 \div 15 = 0.2 \times 100 = 20$

61. 12.5%
$3 \div 24 = 0.125 \times 100 = 12.5$

62. 70%
$58.1 \div 83 = 0.7 \times 100 = 70$

63. 40%
$3.2 \div 8 = 0.4 \times 100 = 40$

64. 40%
$17.6 \div 44 = 0.4 \times 100 = 40$

65. 15%
$6.9 \div 46 = 0.15 \times 100 = 15$

66. 20%
$13.8 \div 69 = 0.2 \times 100 = 20$

67. 25%
$9 \div 36 = 0.25 \times 100$

68. 20%
$4.6 \div 23 =0.2 \times 100$

69. 30%
$3.6 \div 12 = 0.3 \times 100$

70. 16%
$14.4 \div 90 = 0.16 \times 100$

71. 5%
$3.7 \div 74 = 0.05 \times 100$

72. 5%
$2.75 \div 55 = 0.05 \times 100$

73. 90%
    $6.3 \div 7 = 0.9 \times 100$

74. 70%
    $9.8 \div 14 = 0.7 \times 100$

75. 12.5%
    $4.5 \div 36 = 0.125 \times 100$

76. 20% loss
    Percentage loss is calculated as follows: loss divided by buying price
    $3 \div 15 = 0.2 \times 100$

77. 40% profit
    Percentage profit is calculated as follows: profit divided by initial cost
    $12 \div 30 = 0.4 \times 100$

78. 5% profit
    $2 \div 40 = 0.05 \times 100$

79. 91% loss
    $728 \div 800 = 0.91 \times 100$

80. 3% profit
    $2.1 \div 70 = 0.03 \times 100$

81. 42% loss
    $23.1 \div 55 = 0.42 \times 100$

82. 15% profit
    $2.67 \div 17.80 = 0.15 \times 100$

83. 75% loss
    $30.30 \div 40.40 = 0.75 \times 100$

84. 25% profit
    $18.75 \div 75 = 0.25 \times 100$

85. 9% loss
    $9.9 \div 110 = 0.09 \times 100$

86. 60 : 90
    To divide the sum by the ratio: add the values in the ratio together and divide the initial sum by this amount, then calculate the answer by multiplying the ratio values by the result. $2 + 3 = 5$, $150 \div 5 = 30$, $2 \times 30 = 60$, $3 \times 30 = 90$, so the answer is 60 : 90

87. 18 : 72
    $90 \div 5 = 18$, $1 \times 18 = 18$, $4 \times 18 = 72$

88. 84 : 12
    $96 \div 8 = 12$, $12 \times 7 = 84$, $12 \times 1 = 12$

89. 30 : 105
    $135 \div 9 = 15$, $15 \times 2 = 30$, $15 \times 7 = 105$

90. 100 : 80
    $180 \div 9 = 20$, $5 \times 20 = 100$, $4 \times 20 = 80$

91. 78 : 39
    $117 \div 9 = 13$, $13 \times 6 = 78$, $13 \times 3 = 39$

92. 75 : 125
    $200 \div 8 = 25$, $25 \times 3 = 75$, $25 \times 5 = 125$

93. 150 : 100 : 200
    $450 \div 9 = 50$, $50 \times 3 = 150$, $50 \times 2 = 100$, $50 \times 4 = 200$

94. 90 : 135 : 45
    $270 \div 6 = 45$, $45 \times 2 = 90$, $45 \times 3 = 135$, $45 \times 1 = 45$

95. 72 : 56 : 64
    $192 \div 24 = 8$, $8 \times 9 = 72$, $8 \times 7 = 56$, $8 \times 8 = 64$

96. 480 : 180 : 660
$1{,}320 \div 22 = 60, 60 \times 8 = 480, 60 \times 3 = 180, 60 \times 11 = 660$

97. 10 : 30 : 45
$85 \div 17 = 5, 5 \times 2 = 10, 5 \times 6 = 30, 5 \times 9 = 45$

98. 84 : 24 : 60
$168 \div 14 = 12, 12 \times 7 = 84, 12 \times 2 = 24, 12 \times 5 = 60$

99. 24 : 72 : 32
$128 \div 16 = 8, 8 \times 3 = 24, 8 \times 9 = 72, 8 \times 4 = 32$

100. 720 : 900 : 180
$1{,}800 \div 10 = 180, 180 \times 4 = 720, 180 \times 5 = 900, 180 \times 1 = 180$

Test 5: Data interpretation

1. B, 7 : 2
Find the highest common factor (HFC); in this case it is 9, $63 \div 9 = 7$, $18 \div 9 = 2$

2. A, 1 : 2
HCF 27, $27 \div 27 = 1, 54 \div 27 = 2$

3. D, 5 : 3
HCF is 3, $3 \times 5 = 15, 3 \times 3 = 9$

4. D, 9 : 4
HCF = 6, $6 \times 9 = 54, 6 \times 4 = 24$

5. C, 7 : 8
HCF = 4, $4 \times 7 = 28, 4 \times 8 = 32$

6. A, 1 : 3
HCF = 13, $1 \times 13 = 13, 3 \times 13 = 39$

7. D, 2 : 7
   HCF $= 7, 7 \times 2 = 14, 7 \times 7 = 49$

8. B, 5 : 1
   HCF $= 3, 3 \times 5 = 15, 3 \times 1 = 3$

9. C, 6 : 5
   HCF $= 12, 12 \times 6 = 72, 12 \times 5 = 60$

10. D, 4 : 5
    HCF $= 5, 5 \times 4 = 20, 5 \times 5 = 25$

11. B, 3 : 2 : 4
    HCF $= 3, 3 \times 3 = 9, 3 \times 2 = 6, 3 \times 4 = 12$

12. A, 4 : 6 : 1
    HCF $= 5, 5 \times 4 = 20, 5 \times 6 = 30, 5 \times 1 = 5$

13. C, 8 : 2 : 3
    HCF $= 4, 4 \times 8 = 32, 4 \times 2 = 8, 4 \times 3 = 12$

14. B, 5 : 2 : 1
    HCF $= 9, 9 \times 5 = 45, 9 \times 2 = 18, 9 \times 1 = 9$

15. A, 9 : 1 : 5
    HCF $= 6, 6 \times 9 = 54, 6 \times 1 = 6, 6 \times 5 = 30$

16. A, £364
    $4{,}550 \div 100 \times 8$

17. C, £574.34
    $650 \div 100 \times 94 = 611, 611 \div 100 \times 94 = 574.34$

18. C, 60 m
    Treat the stretched carpet as 105%. Work out 100%. $63 \div 105 = 0.6 \times 100 = 60$

19. C, 5 acres
    $3 = 60\%$, so $100\% = 3 \div 60 = 0.05 \times 100 = 5$

20. B, £600
    $690 = 115\%, 690 \div 115 = 6 \times 100 = 600$

21. D, 20%
    $7 \div 35 = 0.2 \times 100 = 20$

22. B, 24%
    £1.20 profit on the two items, $120 \div 500 = 0.24 \times 100 = 24$

23. A, 5%
    5 hours = 300 minutes, $15 \div 300 = 0.05 \times 100 = 5$

24. C, 6%
    3,200 – 3,008 = £192 decrease, $192 \div 3200 = 0.06 \times 100$

25. A, £900
    $112\% = 1{,}008, 1{,}008 \div 112 = 9 \times 100$

26. C, 40%
    $100\% = 3{,}200, 100 \div 3{,}200 \times 1{,}280 = 40$

27. C, 37.5%
    $12 \div 32 = 0.375 \times 100$

28. B, 15%
    $33 \div 220 = 0.15 \times 100$

29. A, 48 grams
    $320 \div 100 \times 15 = 48$

30. C, 30%
    $234{,}000 - 180{,}000 = 54{,}000, 54{,}000 \div 180{,}000 = 0.3 \times 100$

31. B, 7%
    $1{,}750 \div 25{,}000 = 0.07 \times 100$

32. A, 27%
    $3{,}200 - 2{,}336 = 864$, $864 \div 3{,}200 = 0.27 \times 100$

33. D, 96
    $480 \div 100 \times 80 = 384$, $480 - 384 = 96$

34. A, 15,435
    Year 1, $14{,}000 \div 100 \times 5 = 700$, Year 2, $14{,}700 \div 100 \times 5 = 735$, so new population after two years $= 15{,}435$

35. A, £5.60
    $588 = 105\%$, $588 \div 105 = 5.6 \times 100$

36. D, £61.20
    $76.5 \div 100 = 0.765 \times 80 = 61.2$

37. B, 140 grams
    $350 \div 100 = 3.5 \times 40 = 140$

38. C, 19%
    $400 - 324 = 76$, $76 \div 400 = 0.19 \times 100$

39. B, £40,000
    $6\% = 2{,}400$, $1\% = 2{,}400 \div 6 = 400 \times 100 = 40{,}000$

40. A, 60%
    $36.8 - 23 = 13.8$, $13.8 \div 23 = 0.6 \times 100$

41. C, 110%
    $50.4 - 24 = 26.4$, $26.4 \div 24 = 1.1 \times 100 = 110$

42. D, £260
    $7.5\% = 19.5$, $1\% = 19.5 \div 7.5 = 2.6 \times 100 = 260$

43. A, 65%
$7{,}500 = 100\%, 1\% = 7{,}500 \div 100 = 75, 4{,}875 \div 75 = 65$

44. B, 384
$100\% = 480, 1\% = 480 \div 100 = 4.8, 4.8 \times 80 = 80\% = 384$

45. A, 85%
$210 = 100\%, 1\% = 210 \div 100 = 2.1, 210 - 31.5 = 178.5, 178.5 \div 2.1 = 85$

46. D, £350
$106\% = 371, 371 \div 106 = 3.5, 100 \times 3.5 = 350$

47. D, 33%
$1\% = 420, 14{,}000 \div 420 = 33.33$

48. B, 18.75 grams
$125 \div 100 = 1.25 \times 15 = 18.75$

49. C, £2,497.50
$8{,}325 \div 100 = 83.25 \times 30 = 2{,}497.50$

50. A, 3,960
$8{,}800 \div 100 = 88 \times 45 = 3{,}960$

51. B, £18,500
$50{,}000 \div 100 = 500 \times 37 = 18{,}500$

52. C, 17%
$100 \div 250 = 0.4 \times 42.5 = 17$

53. A, 6,450
$7{,}500 \div 100 = 75 \times 86 = 6{,}450$

54. D, £6.48
$1\% = 36.00 \div 100 = 0.36 \times 18 = 6.48$

55. A, 12%
    $4.5 \div 37.5 = 0.12 \times 100 = 12$

56. D, 52.5 grams
    $100\% = 21 \div 40 = 0.525 \times 100 = 52.5$

57. A, 35%
    $1{,}800 \div 100 = 18, 630 \div 18 = 35$

58. B, 80%
    $1\% = 450 \div 100 = 4.5, 360 \div 4.5 = 80$

59. A, 12%
    $20{,}160 - 18{,}000 = 2{,}160, 2{,}160 \div 18{,}000 = 0.12 \times 100$

60. A, 1.32 grams
    $90 \div 15 = 6, 6 \div 100 = 0.06 \times 22 = 1.32$

61. C, £90,000
    $24{,}300 \div 27 = 900, 900 \times 100 = 90{,}000$

62. D, £276
    $15{,}950 - 12{,}500 = 3{,}450, 3{,}450 \div 100 = 34.5 \times 8 = 276$

63. A, Last year
    Last year $63{,}000 \div 630{,}000 = 0.1 \times 100 = 10\%$. This year $6{,}720 \div 84{,}000 = 0.08 \times 100 = 8\%$

64. A, 15%
    Find 66 as a percentage of 440, $440 \div 100 = 4.4, 66 \div 4.4 = 15$

65. C, 200
    45% of 800 are men, so $45 \times 800 = 36{,}000 \div 100 = 360$; 30% are women aged 30 or under, so $30 \times 800 = 24{,}000 \div 100 = 240$; $800 - 360 - 240 = 200$ remaining who must be women over 30

66. D, £8,100
 $6{,}300 \div 7 = 900, 900 \times 9 = 8{,}100$

67. C, 45
 $5 + 3 = 8, 72 \div 8 = 9, 9 \times 5 = 45$

68. A, 64
 $80 \div 5 = 16, 4 \times 16 = 64$

69. B, 200
 $1{,}500 \div 5 = 300, 300 \times 2 = 600, 800 - 600 = 200$

70. C, 40%
 $2 + 3 = 5, 100 \div 5 = 20, 2 \times 20 = 40$

71. A, £800
 Convert the contributions to ratios 3,000 : 4,500 : 10,500 = 3 : 4.5 : 10.5 = 18. We do not use fractions in ratios, so get rid of them by multiplying by 2 = 6 : 9 : 21; this simplifies to 2 : 3 : 7 = 12, $4{,}800 \div 12 = 400$, so investor A receives $2 \times 400 = 800$

72. D, £126
 $5 + 3 = 8, 336 \div 8 = 42, 42 \times 3 = 126$

73. A, £5,000
 900 : 2,700 simplifies to 9 : 27, which in turn simplifies to 1 : 3, $15{,}000 \div 3 = 5{,}000$

74. D, 3 : 2
 Simplifying the ratio gives the answer. Cancelling the zeros gives you 21 : 14; divide both by 7 to obtain the lowest expression 3 : 2

75. A, 28
 You need to establish the equivalent ratio the first value of which is 12. $3 \times 4 = 12$, so the answer is $7 \times 4 = 28$

Test 6: Data interpretation

1. B, 4 : 1
   The sales (largest value) comes first and 72 : 18 simplifies by dividing both by the HCF of 18 to 4 : 1

2. B, 0.05

3. D, 600 kg
   $4 + 2 + 1 = 7, 1{,}050 \div 7 = 150, 150 \times 4 = 600$

4. A, 385
   $7 + 4 = 11, 605 \div 11 = 55, 55 \times 7 = 385$

5. A, 0.14

6. C, 50 : 3
   Ratios should not include fractions or decimals so we must multiply both sides by the same value to remove the decimal. Moving the decimal one place gives 350 : 21; simply divide the HCF by 7 to get 50 : 3

7. D, 0.75

8. C, 8 : 5
   You need to simplify 840 : 525. Do not worry if you cannot quickly work out the HCF (105); just keep dividing both sides to find simpler equivalent ratios until you get down as low as possible. Try 7 and then 15, or 5, 7 and 3

9. B, 0.04

10. B, 1 in 250
    The damage occurred 20 : 5,000, which simplifies to 1 in 250

11. A, 0.24

12. D, £4,500
    The ratio is 3 : 1, £6,000 ÷ 4 = 1,500, 1,500 × 3 = 4,500

13. B, 0.32

14. B, £2,590
    3 + 7 = 10, 3,700 ÷ 10 = 370, 7 × 370 = 2,590

15. B, 0.125

16. C, 4 : 1
    This ratio allows comparisons to be drawn as to the extent to which companies are dependent on outside borrowing. The ratio simplifies to 4 : 1 by dividing both sides by 310,000

17. B, 0.2

18. C, 3 : 5 : 2
    Move the decimal points to make the figures 36 : 60 : 24, divide by the HCF 12 to express the ratio in its simplest form

19. A, 0.64

20. C, 7 : 1
    A percentage can be expressed as a ratio totalling 100, in this case 87.5 : 12.5. The HCF is 12.5 and it simplifies to 7 : 1

21. A, 3 : 2 (in practice it might be expressed as the improper ratio 1.5 : 1)
    The HCF is 14; the ratio describes the company as holding assets of £1.0 for each £1 currently owned

22. C, 0.25

23. D, £198
    6 + 8 = 14, 462 ÷ 14 = 33, 33 × 6 = 198

24. A, 0.25

25. A, 5 : 1 (might be expressed in practice as 5)
The price/earnings ratio is used to evaluate investments. It is a ratio between price and earnings expressed in its simplest form

26. A, 0.175

27. D
The price/earnings ratio of share D is 13 : 1. This means that an investor would have to pay 13 times the last reported earnings for that share. All the others represent better value than this

28. Not less than 370
The cost–benefit figure for road safety schemes is a minimum of 100,000; 37 million ÷ 100,000 = 370

29. 5,070,000,000
3,900 × 1.3 million = 5,070,000,000 or 5 billion and 70 million

30. 1 : 12,500
Passage 1 states that one is 40 times more likely to be killed in an accident in the home than in an air crash and that the chances of dying in an air crash are 1 in 500,000. The chances of dying from an accident in the home are 40 times more than 1 in 500,000. 500,000 ÷ 40 = 12,500

31. 730
Passage 2 states that 10 people die each day on our roads, so in a typical year 3,650 deaths occur, 3,650 ÷ 100 × 20 = 730

32. 6%
234 ÷ 3,900 = 0.06 × 100

33. 264
12% + 28% = 40%, 660 × 40% = 264

34. Funding drug use
    Other reasons saw greater percentage change but apart from buying alcohol (only 4 – 6) all the others were percentage decreases

35. 19%
    $100\% = 42, 8 = 100 \div 42 = 2.38 \times 8 = 19.04 = 19\%$

36. 4 : 1
    Save time calculating the ratios by comparing the percentages. 25% and 23% = 48%; the ratio is therefore 48% : 12%, which can be simplified to 4 : 1 (HCF 12)

37. 14%
    30% fewer respondents = 70% of 660, $660 \div 100 = 6.6 \times 70 = 462$ respondents, 462 = 100%, so 66 respondents = $100 \div 462$ = approx 0.216, $0.216 \times 66 = 14.256$; nearest whole percentage = 14%

38. £115
    $5{,}750 \div 50 = 115$

39. £45
    $1{,}500 + 750 = 2{,}250 \div 50 = 45$

40. 12%
    $128.8 - 115 = 13.8$, $13.8 \div 115 = 0.12 \times 100 = 12$

41. Increase by 210
    The total profit on 50 sets produced at absorption price and sold at the recommended selling price = $128.8 \times 50 - 5{,}750 = 690$, cost of 50 at absorption cost and 50 more at marginal cost = $5{,}750 + 2{,}250 = 8{,}000$, income of 100 sets sold at 89 = 8,900, profit on 50 absorption and 50 marginal sets sold at 89 = 900, profit increased by $900 - 690 = 210$

42. 14%
    Cost is £8,000 (from question 41), profit = $91.20 \times 100 - 8{,}000 = 1{,}120$, % profit = $1{,}120 \div 8{,}000 = 0.14 \times 100 = 14$

43. 55 : 1
    £2.64 : 4.8p = 2,640 : 48, which simplifies to 55 : 1

44. 4%
    19.75 – 18.96 = 0.79, 0.79 ÷ 19.75 = 0.04 × 100 = 4

45. 36%
    Latest figure is given as 1,033 m, increase = 1,033 – 661.12 = 371.88, 371.88 ÷ 1,033 = 0.36 × 100 = 36

46. 15%
    4.8 – 4.08 = 0.72, 0.72 ÷ 4.8 = 0.15 × 100

47. Nil (once the broadband income has been rounded up).
    Fixed line revenue dropped from 4.0 bn to 3.5 bn = –0.5 bn, broadband has increased from 0.6 to 1.1 bn = + 0.5 bn, so net effect is nil

48. 1996
    It can be seen from the graph that the percentage turnout fell from 55.1 to 49.1.

49. 29%
    The cited reasons total 56%, 15% gave no reason, 56 + 15 = 71 leaving 29 from 100

50. 5,150
    The number of votes by men and women can be used. 55% of 5,000 men + 48% of 5,000 women voted pink = 2,750 + 2,400 = 5,150

51. 19 : 26
    Tax as main reason cited received 5% = 500 of respondents, Education = 4% = 400, pink candidate on tax 500 × 56%, on education 400 × 25%, = 380; blue candidate on tax 500 × 44%, on education 400 × 75% = 520, ratio is 380 : 520 which simplifies to 19 : 26

52. 48.97%

We know that the pink candidate received 5,150 votes so the blue candidate received 4,850. Of pink, 48% are graduates, so 5,150 × 48% = 2,472; of blue, 50% of 4,850 = 2,425; total graduates 4,897, as a percentage of 10,000 = 48.97

53. 13

27% of 48 = 48 × 0.27 = 12.96, which rounds up to 13 garages

54. 23

This figure can be taken from the chart, 7 + 8 + 8 = 23

55. £187.50

The mean is found by finding the total of all the charges and dividing that total by the number of charges. 48 garages, 20 franchises and 28 independent, 20 × 282 = 5,640, 28 × 120 = 3,360, 5,640 + 3,360 = 9,000, 9,000 ÷ 48 = 187.5

56. 2 : 3

All 48 garages are classed as either very good, good, below par, poor or very poor. 12 franchised garages are classed as below par or worse so 8 must be classed as very good or good. The ratio then is 8 : 12, which can be simplified as 2 : 3 (HCF 4)

57. 60%

12 out of 20 are below par or worse; to express this as a percentage, calculate 100 ÷ 20 × 12 = 60

58. 16%

All stated percentages total 84, the complete pie chart = 100, other = 100 – 84 = 16

59. £1,450

116 = 8%, 116 ÷ 8 = 14.5 × 100 = 1,450

60. £2,400
    1,800 = 75% of gross income, 100% = 1,800 ÷ 75 = 24 × 100 = 2,400

61. £144
    Other = 16%, 16% of 2,400 = 2,400 ÷ 100 × 16 = 384, 384 ÷ 8 (3 + 4 + 1) = 48, 48 × 3 = 144

62. 4.95% decrease
    33% of 15 = 4.95, so the monthly expenditure will decrease 4.95%

63. 23,668,000 or 23.668 m
    3% less than 2004, 24.4 – 3% = 24.4 ÷ 100 = 0.244 × 3 = 0.732, 24.4 – 0.732 = 23.668

64. 1.6%
    1998 was the previous record with 24 million, 24.4 – 24 = 0.4, 0.4 ÷ 24 = 0.016 × 100 = 1.6%

65. 26.84 bn
    24.4 m × 110 = 2,684 m or 26.84 bn

66. 2.1 m
    30 m × 7% = 30 ÷ 100 × 7 = 2.1

67. 671 bn
    26.84 bn = 4%, 26.84 ÷ 4 = 6.71, 6.71 × 100 = 671 bn

6

Interpretations of your score

Tests 2 and 3: Verbal analysis

A score over 55

If you face a graduate-level psychometric test such as GMAT, LSAT, Fast Stream or SHL and are applying for an oversubscribed position or course, then this is the only category of score that you should be content with.

Your score suggests a high level of ability and confidence in the evaluation of written information. You have demonstrated sustained concentration and an ability to understand quickly fairly complex written argument and to correctly infer its logical consequences.

Concentrate the remaining time you have for further practice on material relevant to other sub-tests so that you can perform to this high standard in all aspects of the challenge.

A score of 40 or above

This is a good score, especially if you secured it in test 2, at your first attempt. If that was the case then take test 3 and try to better it!

In the real test the bulk of candidates are likely to score somewhere in this category. Your score may well be sufficient to get you through to the next stage of the recruitment process. But it will depend on the number of other candidates and vacancies and your precise position in relation to the performance of others.

If you found you did not have sufficient time to complete all the questions then speed up. You might try risking getting a few more wrong because you do not double-check the passage but have more time to attempt all the questions. Alternatively, practise at better managing your time during the test and avoid spending too long on questions that you find difficult.

If you found it hard to maintain the level of concentration demanded by the practice test then this is entirely normal. At the end of a test like this you should feel completely wiped out! If you don't then you are not making the required effort. Remember that even a very able candidate, if they are to do well in a test like this, has to try very hard. Make yourself keep going right until you hear 'Put your pencil down' or the clock runs out of time.

Undertake more practice and see if you can improve that bit more. If you can then you might succeed in pulling yourself further ahead of the majority of candidates and be more sure of a positive result.

A score below 40

Before you take test 3, go over the questions that you got wrong and the explanations and try to work out where you went wrong. It helps to get someone else's opinion. Such a review will greatly assist you to understand the demands of this type of test.

Once you have completed a thorough review, take a break, overnight preferably, and get yourself into a really determined mindset. Find a quiet space and enough time and take test 3, only this time really go for it and practise what you learnt from test 2; prove to yourself that you can do better. You might well be pleasantly surprised with the second result. If you manage a better score on your second attempt then you have made an important discovery. You have realized that you have what it takes to do well in these tests and you have realized what you have to do to do well in these tests.

Now set aside a quite significant amount of time for further practice. Seek out other titles in the Kogan Page Testing Series containing this sort of question, and make it a habit to read a quality newspaper every day and economic and political weekly journals.

Take encouragement from the fact that with practice you can show dramatic improvements in your score in this type of sub-test. In time you will gain further in confidence, accuracy and speed. It will take time but if the opportunity towards which you are working is something you really want, then simply go for it. You have already begun the process of dramatically improving your score, so take encouragement. The vast majority of candidates will discover that they need more practice the hard way by failing a real test. You are already ahead of them so track down sufficient practice material on which to work and get started in plenty of time.

Test 4: Data interpretation

A score over 80

If you obtained this score in the minimum allowed time then you succeeded in demonstrating speed, accuracy, confidence and familiarity in these key operations. Go on to the further tests knowing that you made a very good start. If you face a graduate psychometric test in highly competitive circumstances then realize that this is really the only score you can afford to be happy with.

If you gave yourself the maximum time allowed then still be encouraged with your result. Take confidence from it. Try the other tests, allowing yourself less time. A high degree of competence in these key operations will serve you very well in a real test. For some candidates it will mean the difference between pass and fail.

A score of 60 or above

In a real test the bulk of candidates are likely to score somewhere in this category and your score may well be sufficient to get you through to the next stage of the recruitment process.

While it is a good test score, it could be better and to be sure of a positive result you should practise more. Establish which principles were involved in the questions that you got wrong and start a programme of practice that begins with the revision of these operations.

Once you have become more confident in these and all the operations tested then undertake test 5 and try to beat your score, only this time consider allowing yourself less time per question.

If you ran out of time before you were able to complete all the questions then review your mental arithmetic and set about a programme of practice to become faster and more confident in it. Everyone finds this hard work, boring, painful even, but if you really want to succeed in the numeracy part of graduate psychometric tests then there is no alternative. The good news is that you are guaranteed to get a lot better really fast – it merely takes hard work and determination!

A score below 60

If maths is something you have previously managed without, then now is the time to address this imbalance. There is really no point in allowing yourself to be rejected as a great candidate except for the maths. This is the fate of many candidates and one you risk if you do not set about a major programme of revision.

If you found you did not have sufficient time to complete all the questions then speed up! Achieve this through practice, practice and some more practice of your mental arithmetic. Drive yourself half mad by posing and answering simple multiplications in your head, move on to simple percentages and do not stop until you can complete the type of sum in this first test accurately and quickly. Once you have reached this point, take test 5 and prove to yourself how much you have improved. Practise at better managing your time during the test and avoid spending too long on questions that you find difficult.

If you found it hard to maintain the level of concentration demanded by the practice test then this is entirely normal. At the end of a test like this you should feel completely wiped out! If you don't, then you are not making the required effort. The alternative is to practise your mental arithmetic until you are able to do a test like this without expending such concentration.

Undertake more practice before you take the next test and then really go for it and see if you can improve on your first score.

Tests 5 and 6: Data interpretation

A score over 54

In a graduate-level psychometric test such as GMAT, LSAT, Fast Stream or SHL and where the test is being used to select between many more candidates than there are positions or places, this is the category of score you must realize.

If you obtained this score in the minimum allowed time then you have continued to demonstrate the necessary speed, accuracy, confidence and familiarity in these key operations. Once you have done all three tests, concentrate the remaining time before your real test on further practising on material relevant to more advanced numerical operations and other sub-tests so that you can perform to this high standard in all aspects of the challenge.

If you gave yourself the maximum time allowed in test 5 then you should also be encouraged by your result and should consider trying test 6 in the minimum time allowed.

When you have completed the material in this book, go on to more advanced numerical practice material in order that you can maximize the advantage you enjoy. Suitable material is available in the Kogan Page titles *How to Pass Advanced Numeracy Tests* and *Advanced Numeracy Tests Workbook.*

A score of 40 or above

It is a good test score and many candidates who score in this category will pass the numerical sub-tests of the challenge they face. But you should practise more to be sure of a positive result in a real test. Establish which fundamentals were involved in any questions that you got wrong and start a programme of practice that begins with the revision of these operations.

Remember that the operations being examined in these practice tests represent the minimum competencies required for this type of test. So keep improving your mental arithmetic and keep practising so that your numerical reasoning skills continue to improve.

Do not be surprised if you found it hard to maintain the level of concentration demanded by the practice test; most people do. Even the numerically talented have to try really hard to do well in graduate psychometric tests. At the end of a test like this you should feel completely wiped out! If you still have test 6 to go then take a break, overnight preferably, and get yourself into a really determined mindset. Find a quiet space and enough time and take the last test, only this time really go for it and practise what you have learnt; prove to yourself that you can do better.

A score below 40

Continue and extend your efforts to revise your mental arithmetic. Consider undertaking one hour's practice a day over the next three weeks. When travelling on a bus or train, when out for a walk, pose and answer simple sums to yourself. I knew a candidate who used to add up the numbers on each car number plate he passed, then he multiplied each number of the car registration plates. He kept this up until he was able to do the calculation before he arrived at the next car. Try it; it worked for him. Another determined candidate purchased a pile of mental arithmetic revision textbooks intended for schoolchildren – they comprise pages and pages of practice questions in the basic operations (you will find them in most bookshops). He worked on these for weeks until his speed and accuracy were such that he was able to take his basic maths for granted and concentrate instead on evaluating the data presented and the more complex numerical reasoning that the test demanded.

Go over your answers and identify the type of question you got wrong. Use the explanations to establish where you are going wrong. Ask someone to help. Seek out further examples of these questions and practise them until you have mastered them. You will find suitable practice information in the Kogan Page titles *How to Pass Numeracy Tests* and *How to Pass Numerical Reasoning Tests*. When you have mastered these titles, put yourself through the tests in this book all over again.

Don't give up; just keep practising at getting right these essential operations and building up your speed, accuracy and confidence. You are guaranteed to get a lot better really fast – it merely takes hard work and determination!

Further reading from Kogan Page

Books

The Advanced Numeracy Test Workbook, Mike Bryon, 2003

Aptitude, Personality and Motivation Tests: Assess Your Potential and Plan Your Career, 2nd edition, Jim Barrett, 2004

The Aptitude Test Workbook, Jim Barrett, 2003

Great Answers to Tough Interview Questions: How to Get the Job You Want, 6th edition, Martin John Yate, 2005

How to Master Personality Questionnaires, 2nd edition, Mark Parkinson, 2000

How to Master Psychometric Tests, 3rd edition, Mark Parkinson, 2004

How to Pass Advanced Aptitude Tests, Jim Barrett, 2002

How to Pass the Civil Service Qualifying Tests, 2nd edition, Mike Bryon, 2003

How to Pass Computer Selection Tests, Sanjay Modha, 1994

How to Pass Firefighter Recruitment Tests, Mike Bryon, 2004

How to Pass Graduate Psychometric Tests, 2nd edition, Mike Bryon, 2001

How to Pass the New Police Selection System, 2nd edition, Harry Tolley, Billy Hodge and Catherine Tolley, 2004

How to Pass Numeracy Tests, 2nd edition, Harry Tolley and Ken Thomas, 2000

How to Pass Numerical Reasoning Tests, Heidi Smith, 2003

How to Pass Professional Level Psychometric Tests, 2nd edition, Sam Al-Jajjoka, 2004

How to Pass Selection Tests, 3rd edition, Mike Bryon and Sanjay Modha, 2005
How to Pass Technical Selection Tests, Mike Bryon, 2005
How to Pass Verbal Reasoning Tests, 2nd edition, Harry Tolley and Ken Thomas, 2000
IQ and Psychometric Test Workbook, Philip Carter, 2005
Preparing Your Own CV: How to Improve Your Chances of Getting the Job You Want, 3rd edition, Rebecca Corfield, 2003
Readymade CVs: Sample CVs for Every Type of Job, 3rd edition, Lynn Williams, 2004
Readymade Job Search Letters: Every Type of Letter for Getting the Job You Want, 3rd edition, Lynn Williams, 2004
Successful Interview Skills, Rebecca Corfield, 1992
Test Your Own Aptitude, 3rd edition, Jim Barrett and Geoff Williams, 2003
The Ultimate Interview Book, Lynn Williams, 2005

CD ROMS

Psychometric Tests, Volume 1, The Times Testing Series, Editor Mike Bryon 2002
Test Your Aptitude, Volume 1, The Times Testing Series, Editor Mike Bryon, 2002
Test Your IQ, Volume 1, The Times Testing Series, Editor Mike Bryon, 2002